Welcome to
Table Talk

C000265276

Table Talk helps children and adults explore the Bible together. Each day provides a short family Bible time which, with your own adaptation, could work for ages 4 to 12. It includes optional follow-on material which takes the passage further for older children. There are also suggestions for linking **Table Talk** with **XTB** children's notes.

Who can use Table Talk?

Table Talk

A short family Bible time for daily use. Table Talk takes about five minutes, maybe at breakfast, or after an evening meal. Choose whatever time and place suits you best as a family. Table Talk includes a simple discussion starter or activity that leads into a short Bible reading. This is followed by a few questions.

- **Families**
- **One adult with one child**
- **A teenager with a younger brother or sister**
- **Children's leaders with their groups**
- **Any other mix that works for you!**

XTB

XTB children's notes help 7-11 year olds to get into the Bible for themselves. They are based on the same Bible passages as **Table Talk**. You will find suggestions for how **XTB** can be used alongside **Table Talk** on the next page.

In the next three pages you'll find suggestions for how to use Table Talk, along with hints and tips for adapting it to your own situation. If you've never done anything like this before, check out our web page for further help (see website addresses below) or write in for a fact sheet.

THE SMALL PRINT

Table Talk is published by The Good Book Company, Blenheim House, 1 Blenheim Road, Epsom, Surrey, KT19 9AP, UK
Written by Alison Mitchell (alison@thegoodbook.co.uk) and Mark Tomlinson. Fab pictures by Kirsty McAllister. Bible quotations taken from the Good News Bible. **UK:** www.thegoodbook.co.uk **North America:** www.thegoodbook.com
Australia: www.thegoodbook.com.au **New Zealand:** www.thegoodbook.co.nz

HOW TO USE
Table Talk

Table Talk is designed to last for up to three months. How you use it depends on what works for you. We have included 65 full days of material in this issue, p[...] some more low-key suggestions for another 26 days (at the back of the book). We would like to encoura[...] you to work at establishing a pattern of family readi[...] The first two weeks are the hardest!

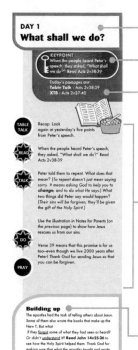

DAY 1
What shall we do?

> **KEYPOINT**
> When the people heard Peter's speech, they asked, "What shall we do?" Read Acts 2v38-39

Today's passages are:
Table Talk : Acts 2v38-39
XTB : Acts 2v37-40

TABLE TALK — Recap: Look again at yesterday's five points from Peter's speech.

READ — When the people heard Peter's speech, they asked, "What shall we do?" Read Acts 2v38-39

TALK — Peter told them to repent. What does that mean? (To repent doesn't just mean saying sorry. It means asking God to help you to *change*, and to do what He says.) What two things did Peter say would happen? (Their sins will be forgiven, they'll be given the gift of the Holy Spirit.)

DO — Use the illustration in Notes for Parents (on the previous page) to show how Jesus rescues us from our sins.

PRAY — Verse 39 means that this promise is for us too—even though we live 2000 years after Peter! Thank God for sending Jesus so that you can be forgiven.

Building up
The apostles had the task of telling others about Jesus. Some of them also wrote the books that make up the New T. But what
if they *forgot* some of what they had seen or heard? Or didn't *understand* it? Read John 14v25-26 to see how the Holy Spirit helped them. Thank God for making sure that what the apostles taught and wrote down about Jesus was true and accurate.

Table Talk is based on the same Bible passages as *XTB*, but usually only asks for two or three verses to be read out loud. The full *XTB* passage is listed at the top of each Table Talk page. If you are using Table Talk with older children, read the full *XTB* passage rather than the shorter version.

The main part of Table Talk is designed to be suitable for younger children. *Building Up* includes more difficult questions designed for older children, or those with more Bible knowledge.

As far as possible, if your children are old enough to read the Bible verses for themselves, encourage them to find the answers in the passage and to tell you which verse the answer is in. This will help them to get used to handling the Bible for themselves.

The Building Up section is optional. It is designed to build on the passage studied in Table Talk (and XTB). Building Up includes some additional questions which reinforce the main teaching point, apply the teaching more directly, or follow up any difficult issues raised by the passage.

> **KEYPOINT**
> This is the main point you should be trying to convey. Don't read this out—it often gives away the end of the story!

Linking with *XTB*

The XTB children's notes are based on the same passages as Table Talk. There are a number of ways in which you can link the two together:
- Children do XTB on their own. Parents then follow these up later (see suggestions below).
- A child and adult work through XTB together.
- A family uses Table Talk together at breakfast. Older children then use XTB on their own later.
- You use Table Talk on its own, with no link to XTB.

FOLLOWING UP XTB

If your child uses XTB on their own it can be helpful to ask them later to show you (or tell you) what they've done. Some useful starter questions are:

- Can you tell me what the reading was about?
- Is there anything you didn't understand or want to ask about?

- Did anything surprise you in the reading? Was there anything that would have surprised the people who first saw it or read about it?

- What did you learn about God, Jesus or the Holy Spirit?
- Is there anything you're going to do as a result of reading this passage?

Table Talk is deliberately not too ambitious. Most families find it quite hard to set up a regular pattern of reading the Bible together—and when they do meet, time is often short. So **Table Talk** is designed to be quick and easy to use, needing little in the way of extra materials, apart from pen and paper now and then.

BUT!!

Most families have special times when they **can** be more ambitious, or do have some extra time available. Here are some suggestions for how you can use **Table Talk** as the basis for a special family adventure...

PICNIC

Take Table Talk with you on a family picnic. Thank God for His beautiful Creation.

WALK

Go for a walk together. Stop somewhere with a good view and read Genesis 1v1–2v4.

GETTING TOGETHER

Invite another family for a meal, and to read the Bible together. The children could make a poster based on the passage.

MUSEUM

Visit a museum to see a display from Bible times. Use it to remind yourselves that the Bible tells us about real people and real history.

HOLIDAYS

Set aside a special time each day while on holiday. Choose some unusual places to read the Bible together—on the beach, up a mountain, in a boat... Take some photos to put on your Table Talk display when you get back from holiday.

You could try one of the special holiday editions of XTB and Table Talk—Christmas Unpacked, Easter Unscrambled and Summer Signposts.

Have an adventure!

FOOD!

Eat some food linked with the passage you are studying. For example Manna (biscuits made with honey, Exodus 16v31), Unleavened bread or Honeycomb (Matthew 3v4—but don't try the locusts!)

DISPLAY AREA

We find it easier to remember and understand what we learn when we have something to look at. Make a Table Talk display area, for pictures, Bible verses and prayers. Add to it regularly.

VIDEO

A wide range of Bible videos are available—from simple cartoon stories, to whole Gospels filmed with real life actors. (Your local Christian bookshop should have a range.) Choose one that ties in with the passages you are reading together. **_Note:_** Use the video in addition to the Bible passage, not instead of it!

PRAYER DIARY

As a special project, make a family prayer diary. Use it to keep a note of things you pray for—and the answers God gives you. This can be a tremendous help to children (and parents!) to learn to trust God in prayer as we see how He answers over time.

Go on—try it!

DRAMA OR PUPPETS

Take time to dramatise a Bible story. Maybe act it out (with costumes if possible) or make some simple puppets to retell the story.

Enough of the introduction, let's get going...

Notes for Parents

MARK'S GOSPEL

Gospel means "good news". Mark's book tells us the good news about Jesus. It's divided into two halves...

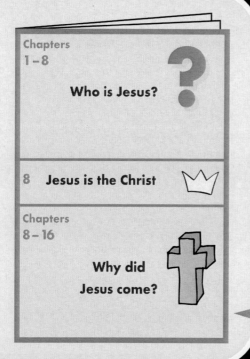

Chapters 1–8	Who is Jesus?
8	Jesus is the Christ
Chapters 8–16	Why did Jesus come?

MEET MARK

We can meet Mark in the book of Acts. He was Barnabas' cousin. He had two names—John and Mark. Sometimes he was called John Mark, sometimes just Mark or John! When Peter was in prison, the Christians met to pray for him in Mark's mum's house (Acts 12v12). Mark joined Paul and Barnabas on a journey to tell people about Jesus. Later, Mark travelled just with Barnabas. (Acts 15v36-39)

When Mark wrote his book, he wrote it in a language called Greek. It looks like this: αλισον μιτχηελλ. Mark's book didn't have chapters and verses—or headings. These were added later to make it easier for us to find our way around the book.

Mark time

> **KEYPOINT**
> Mark's Gospel tells us the good news about **Jesus**—God's chosen King, the Son of God.

Today's passages are:
Table Talk: Mark 1v1
XTB: Mark 1v1

TABLE TALK

Imagine someone comes for dinner, and brings a friend called Bill. Before dinner he says to you, "I'd like you to meet my friend, Bill. Actually, Bill is God!" What would you think? (*That your friend is joking? Or crazy? Or that you'd want some evidence?*)

READ

That's similar to how Mark starts his book. He introduces us to Jesus, and tells us that Jesus is God! **Read Mark 1v1**

TALK

What are the two titles Mark gives to Jesus? (*Christ, Son of God*).

Christ isn't Jesus' surname. He wasn't called Mr. Christ! The title *Christ* is a Greek Word. (The same title in Hebrew is *Messiah*.) It means "God's Chosen King".

Mark is telling us that Jesus is the <u>King</u>, and that He's <u>God</u>. Those are amazing claims! The first half of Mark's book gives **evidence** for these claims and shows why Mark believes them.

Look at the diagram in **Notes for Parents** to see how Mark divides his book into two halves.

DO

(*Optional*) Make a copy of the diagram, and stick it up where you can all see it.

PRAY

Ask God to help you to learn more about who Jesus is and why He came as you read Mark's book together.

Building up
Find out more about
Mark in **Notes for Parents**
opposite.

Royal messenger

The king is coming

KEYPOINT
John the Baptist was the promised messenger, to get people ready for the King.

Today's passages are:
Table Talk: Mark 1v2-5
XTB: Mark 1v2-6

KEYPOINT
John tells people that the coming King is far greater than him, and will baptise with the Holy Spirit.

Today's passages are:
Table Talk: Mark 1v6-8
XTB: Mark 1v6-8

TABLE TALK

(*You need paper and pencil.*) Draw three stick men, labelled King, Rescuer and Messenger. Ask your child to add details to each picture to show that they are a <u>King</u> (e.g. crown and cloak), a <u>Rescuer</u> (e.g. fireman's helmet and hose) and <u>Messenger</u> (e.g. mail bag).

READ

In the Old Testament, God promised to send a new **King**, who would also be a **Rescuer**. But first, God would send a **Messenger**, to tell the people to get ready for the King. Listen to see which promise God keeps in today's reading. **Read Mark 1v2-5**

TALK

Which promise did God keep? (*To send a messenger.*) Who came as the messenger? (v4) (*John the Baptist.*) John knew that the people weren't ready for their King. They hadn't been living the way God wanted them to. So what did John tell them to do? (v4-5) (*To repent/turn away from their sins, and to be baptised.*) When John baptised people, it showed that they wanted to be washed clean from all their wrongs (their sins) ready to welcome King Jesus.

PRAY

God sent John as His messenger—just as He had promised. Thank God that He <u>always</u> keeps His promises.

Building up
Mark quotes two Old Testament prophets in v2-3. (*It was common only to name the most important one, in this case Isaiah.*) Read the original prophecies in **Malachi 3v1** and **Isaiah 40v3-5.**

TABLE TALK

Guess that Job: Give clues to someone's job by describing (or drawing) the clothes they would wear. E.g. a nurse, chef, policeman, astronaut, judge, postman...

READ

The Old Testament promises about the royal messenger say that he will be like **Elijah**. He was an Old Testament *prophet* (God's messenger) who wore hair clothing with a leather belt. Listen for this as you read about John the Baptist. **Read Mark 1v6-8**

TALK

What did John wear and eat? (See v6.) Who did he look like? (*Elijah—evidence that he's the promised messenger.*) John told the people about **Jesus**, the coming King. What did he say about Jesus? (v7-8) (*Jesus is greater than John; Jesus will baptise with the Holy Spirit.*)

THINK

When **John** baptised people, what part of them did he wash? (*The outside.*) But what would **Jesus** baptise with? (v8) (*The Holy Spirit.*) Jesus would give His Spirit to His followers, to live <u>in them</u> and help them to live for Him.

PRAY

At another time, John said this about Jesus: *"He must become greater; I must become less."* (John 3v30) Mark's book will show us how great Jesus is. Ask God to help you to see Jesus' greatness more as you read Mark.

Building up
Read more of what John said about Jesus in **John 3v22-30.** John says he is like a best man, waiting for the bridegroom. His joy is complete when the groom (Jesus) arrives.

TALKING ABOUT BAPTISM

For young children, it probably won't be appropriate to get involved with discussions about the purpose of baptism. Keep it simple, and just ensure that they understand what John actually did (especially if they have only seen babies "sprinkled"). The picture opposite will help them to understand that John completely submerged people in a river. (He dunked them!)

With older children, talk about what baptism is a sign of, as explained below...

Inside Outside

Is baptism the same as having a bath? Why / why not?

Being **baptised** is like being washed clean on the <u>outside</u>. Being **forgiven** is like being washed clean on the <u>inside</u>. Baptism is an outside sign of an inside change.

John could only wash people clean on the <u>outside</u>—like giving them a bath. Only **one** person can make us clean on the <u>inside</u>. Who?

WHY WAS JESUS BAPTISED?

The people who came to John to be baptised admitted that they were sinful and needed to be forgiven. John baptised **sinners** who **repented** (turned away from their sins).

But *Jesus* was very different. He lived a **perfect** life. He <u>never</u> sinned, and had no need to repent. Jesus was baptised to **please** God. It was all part of God's plan for Him.

Note: Even John found it hard to understand why Jesus was baptised. John knew that <u>he</u> was the sinful one, not Jesus! Read their conversation in **Matthew 3v13-15**. Jesus' answer shows that being baptised was part of God's plan for Him. He obeyed His Father.

KEYPOINT

Jesus is God's loved Son, who came to rescue us. He was baptised to please God.

Today's passages are:
Table Talk: Mark 1v9-11
XTB: Mark 1v9-11

TABLE TALK

Talk about any experience of baptism your child has had or seen. If they have been baptised themselves, talk about what happened (and show a photo if you can). If you're waiting until they are older, talk about why.

READ

When John baptised people, he did it in the Jordan River. They went right under the water and up again. Read about what happened when Jesus came to be baptised. **Read Mark 1v9-11**

TALK

What happened when Jesus came up out of the water? (v10-11) (*The dove came down, and God spoke.*)

DO

Finish the picture by drawing a dove, and a speech bubble saying "You are my Son."

What three things did God say about Jesus? (v11) (*Jesus is His Son; He loves Him; He's pleased with Him.*)

PRAY

Pray for anyone you know who has just been or soon will be baptised.

Building up

Use **Notes for Parents** opposite to think some more about baptism.

DAY 5
Tempting times

KEYPOINT
Jesus was tempted, but never sinned. God promises to help us when tempted.

Today's passages are:
Table Talk: Mark 1v12-13
XTB: Mark 1v12-13

TABLE TALK

Which of these have you ever been <u>tempted</u> to do? (Lying, stealing, gossiping, swearing, being greedy.) *It's important that everyone is honest here, adults as well as children.*

READ

Jesus knows what it's like to be tempted.
Read Mark 1v12-13

TALK

Who sent Jesus into the desert? (v12) (*The Holy Spirit.*) How long was Jesus there? (v13) (*40 days.*) Who was with Him? (v13) (*Satan/the devil, wild animals, angels.*)

THINK

Satan (the devil) always wants to <u>spoil</u> God's good plans. He would try anything to stop Jesus, because Jesus is God's chosen King, who had come to rescue His people. But Jesus is perfect! He didn't give in to the tempter.

WOW!

Satan is sometimes called the <u>tempter</u>. He tempts us to do things which displease God—and is delighted when we give in. But the Bible promises that **God** will always help us when tempted! He will give us a way out. (*You can read this promise in 1 Corinthians 10v13.*)

PRAY

Talk to God about this. Ask Him to help you when tempted.

Building up
Read the story of Jesus' temptations in more detail in **Matthew 4v1-11**. How does Jesus respond to each temptation? (*By quoting God's words from the Old Testament.*) How could Jesus' example help <u>you</u> when you're being tempted? Pray about it together.

DAY 6
The time has come

KEYPOINT
The Kingdom of God is near, because Jesus the King has arrived.

Today's passages are:
Table Talk: Mark 1v14-15
XTB: Mark 1v14-15

TABLE TALK

Find these places on the map:
- Where Jesus was <u>born</u> (*Bethlehem*)

- Where He <u>grew up</u> (*Nazareth*)
- Where He was <u>baptised</u> by John (*Jordan river*)
- Where He was <u>tempted</u> (*the desert*).

READ

Now Jesus is going to **Galilee**. Find it on the map, then read **Mark 1v14-15**

TALK

What happened to John? (v14) (*He was put in prison.*) What did Jesus say had <u>come</u>? (v15) (*The right time.*) What was <u>near</u>? (*The kingdom of God.*) What must people do? (*Repent and believe.*)

THINK

The Kingdom of God isn't a **place**—like Scotland or New Zealand! It's **people**, who have Jesus as their King, ruling over them. The Kingdom of God is <u>near</u> because Jesus the King has arrived. So people must **repent** (turn away from sin) and **believe** the good news about Jesus.

PRAY

Thank God for keeping His promise to send Jesus as King.

Building up
When Jesus went to Galilee, it fulfilled what the Old Testament had said about Him. **Read Matthew 4v12-17**. Nothing Jesus did was by accident! It was all in God's plan.

DAY 7
Follow me

KEYPOINT
Jesus has authority over people. He called these fishermen to be "fishers of men".

Today's passages are:
Table Talk: Mark 1v16-20
XTB: Mark 1v16-20

TABLE TALK

(*Optional!*) Take it in turns to pretend to creep round behind someone and catch them in a large net!

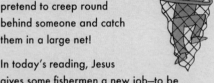

READ

In today's reading, Jesus gives some fishermen a new job—to be "fishers of men". What do you think that means? (*To tell people about Jesus the King.*) **Read Mark 1v16-20**

TALK

Who did Jesus call to follow Him? (v16&19) (*Simon [Peter], Andrew, James, John.*) What was their new job? (*To be fishers of men, by telling them about Jesus.*) How quickly did these men go with Jesus? (v18&20) (*At once.*)

THINK

In the next few days we'll see Jesus' amazing authority. *He's in charge!* Mark will show us that Jesus has the same authority as God—evidence that Jesus **is** the Son of God. Today's story shows that Jesus has authority over **people**.

Notes for Parents (opposite) gives details of an *Evidence Chart* to make. If you don't have time now, try and make it later so that you can add to it over the next few days.

DO

PRAY

These men followed Jesus all their lives, and told others about Him too. Are you followers of Jesus? Do you want to tell your friends about Him? Pray together about your answers.

Building up
Imagine if you had been one of those fishermen. Do you think you would have left your job and gone with Jesus? Why / why not?

EVIDENCE CHART   (DAY 7)
In the first half of Mark's book, He is giving us **evidence** for who Jesus is. (See the diagram on Day 1.) In the next few days we will see evidence that Jesus has the same authority as **God**—because He is the Son of God.

Make a chart like the one below. Start it today, and add to it over the next few days. With older children, add the Bible reference as well.

EVIDENCE CHART

Jesus is in charge—He has the same authority as God

- Authority over **people**. (Mark 1v16-20)
- Authority as a _____
- Authority over _____
- Authority over _____
- Authority to _____

JESUS IN THE SYNAGOGUE   (DAY 8)
Jesus went to the Jewish meeting place (the synagogue). When He began to teach the people they were amazed, because He taught with such authority! But there was a man there who had an evil spirit living in him. He shouted at Jesus, "What do you want with us? Have you come to destroy us? I know who you are—you're the Holy One of God!" "Be quiet!" said Jesus. "Come out of the man!" The evil spirit shook the man hard, gave a loud scream, and came out of him.

(Based on Mark 1v21-26)

Who's in charge?

KEYPOINT
Jesus has authority as a teacher and over evil spirits.

Today's passages are:
Table Talk: Mark 1v21-28
XTB: Mark 1v21-28

TABLE TALK

Look back at yesterday's Evidence Chart. What kind of authority did Jesus have? (*Over people*.) How quickly did the fishermen follow Jesus? (*At once*.) In today's reading Jesus' shows two more kinds of authority...

READ

*With older children, read the whole passage—***Mark 1v21-28**

*With younger children, read the story summary in **Notes for Parents**, and then read* **Mark 1v27-28**

TALK

What kinds of authority did Jesus show in this story? (v22 & 26) (*Authority as a **teacher**—v22, Authority over **evil spirits**—v26*).

DO

Add both of these to your Evidence Chart.

How did the people feel about Jesus? (v27) (*Amazed*)

PRAY

What Jesus <u>did</u> was amazing—and so was what He <u>taught</u>. As you read Mark's book, you'll be reading more of Jesus' amazing teaching for yourselves. Ask God to help you to understand Jesus' teaching, and to do what He says.

Building up

Sometimes in the Bible we read about evil spirits. They are God's enemies, and often made people ill. But **God** is <u>far</u> more powerful than any evil spirit! When Jesus commanded the evil spirit to leave the man, what happened? (v26) (*It left at once*.) The evil spirit <u>had</u> to obey Jesus. Jesus is **in charge!** (*If they are worried, reassure your child that there's nothing to worry about. They cannot be "possessed" if Jesus is their King. Jesus is far more powerful than the power of evil*.)

Nay fever!

KEYPOINT
Jesus has authority over sickness.

Today's passages are:
Table Talk: Mark 1v29-31
XTB: Mark 1v29-34

TABLE TALK

Yesterday's story and today's both happened in the same town. Check back to verse 21 to see which town it was. (*Capernaum*)
Find it on the map on Day 6.

READ

Capernaum was a fishing village on the shore of the Sea of Galilee. Simon and Andrew lived there. When they left the synagogue (yesterday's story), they took Jesus to their home.
Read Mark 1v29-31

TALK

Who was ill? (v30) (*Simon's mother-in-law*.) What was wrong with her? (*She had a fever*.) What did Jesus do? (*See v31*) How do we know that she was completely better? (v31) (*She was able to get up and look after them all*.)

THINK

This story shows another kind of <u>authority</u>. What does Jesus have authority over? (*Sickness*) Only **God** has complete control over sickness. But Jesus had the <u>same</u> authority—because He is the **Son of God**.

DO

Add "Authority over sickness" to your Evidence Chart.

Pray for anyone you know who is ill.

PRAY

Building up

Read about what happened that evening in **Mark 1v32-34**. Which two kinds of authority did Jesus show? (*Over sickness and over demons/evil spirits*.) Why do you think He wouldn't let the demons say who He was? (*See 1v14-15 for a clue about Jesus' priorities. More about that tomorrow*.)

DAY 10 Praying and preaching

TABLE TALK

Two weeks ago I went to a friend's birthday party—at quarter to seven in the morning!! Do you ever get up really early for something? What for? (*E.g. an early start when you're going on holiday, to open your Christmas stocking...*)

READ

In today's story, Jesus gets up really early—but it's not for a party! **Read Mark 1v35-39**

TALK

Why did Jesus get up so early? (v35) (*To go and pray.*) Simon and the others had to search for Jesus. What did they say when they found Him? (v37) ("*Everyone is looking for you!*")

Think back to yesterday's story. Why do you think everyone's looking for Jesus. (*Probably to see more miracles.*) But Jesus wouldn't stay in Capernaum. He had to visit other towns as well. Why? (v38) (*To preach.*)

THINK

Prayer <u>mattered</u> to Jesus. It was more important than sleeping in! When do <u>you</u> pray? Do you find it hard to find time? Would you get up early to pray—even if you were tired? When is a good time to pray together? And on your own?

PRAY

Ask God to help you to spend time talking to Him **every day**.

Building up

In verse 38 Jesus says that He has come to preach. Look back to **Mark 1v14-15** to see what Jesus was preaching. The crowds wanted to see miracles. Why do you think it was more important to preach to them? (*Their greatest need was to turn away from their sin and believe the good news about Jesus.*)

DAY 11 Miracle man

TABLE TALK

Have you ever been ill with something catching, like Chicken Pox? How did you feel? What difference did it make that it was catching? (*E.g. your friends couldn't come to visit.*)

READ

In Bible times, people sometimes caught a horrible skin disease called **leprosy**. It was <u>very</u> catching, so you had to leave your home and friends. You could <u>never</u> come back—unless the priests checked you and said you were no longer ill. **Read Mark 1v40-42**

TALK

What did the man with leprosy want Jesus to do? (v40) (*Make him well. If he was cured, he would be "clean" and so allowed to return to his home, and also to the synagogue to praise God.*) How did Jesus feel about him? (v41) (*He cared about him/was full of compassion/pity.*) What did Jesus do? (v42) (*Healed him.*) What **authority** was Jesus showing? (*Authority over sickness.*)

PRAY

In some countries, leprosy is still a big problem today—especially in India, Brazil and Indonesia. Pray for **The Leprosy Mission**, a Christian charity, and for the people they help. You can find out more at www.leprosymission.org

Building up

Jesus cured this man, but there was a price to pay. **Read Mark 1v43-45** Jesus told the man just to go to the priest to be checked, but not to tell anyone else. But what did the man do? (v45) (*Told everyone.*) What was the result? (*See v45.*) As we saw yesterday, Jesus came to **preach**. But now He has to stay away from the towns because of the crowds.

DAY 12
Down he came...

DAY 12
Notes for Parents

KEYPOINT
Everyone's biggest problem is **Sin**.

Today's passages are:
Table Talk: Mark 2v1-5
XTB: Mark 2v1-5

DO

If possible, find a small box to use as a model of a Bible house, and draw in a door and stairs to the roof. Otherwise, draw a picture like the one here.

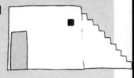

READ

In today's story, Jesus was <u>inside</u> a house like this. He was teaching, and huge crowds had come to hear Him. They were squashed into every corner, and spilled out into the road outside as well! Then some men came, carrying their paralysed friend on a mat. But there was no room to get in...
Read Mark 2v1-5

TALK

How did the men get their friend to Jesus? (*See v4. Bible houses had flat roofs with tiles laid over branches, so it was possible to pull these up to make a hole.*) These men had gone to a lot of effort to reach Jesus! What do you think they wanted Him to do? (*Heal their friend.*) But what did Jesus actually say? (v5) (*"Your sins are forgiven."*)

Use **Notes for Parents** to see why *sin* was this man's biggest problem.

PRAY

Thank God for sending Jesus die in our place, as our ransom, so that we can be forgiven.

Building up
Look up further Bible verses describing Jesus as our *ransom* (or the one who *redeems* us): Ephesians 1v7; 1 Peter 1v18-19; Revelation 5v9.

RANSOMING SLAVES
Imagine you are in a slave-market, and that your children are slaves! Give them each a sheet of paper that says *Slave*, and with a high price on it. (E.g. £1000) The only way they can be set free is if the price is paid. This money is called the **ransom**. Do they have the money? (No!) So what is the only way they can be free? (*If <u>someone else</u> pays the ransom for them.*)

Jesus is our Ransom
Now look at what Jesus says later in Mark's book. ("Son of Man" is a title Jesus often used for Himself.)

"The Son of Man did not come to be served, but to serve, and to give his life as a ransom for many." (Mark 10v45)

Why is Jesus using the language of the slave market? Because we are all slaves! We are slaves of **sin**—and there's <u>nothing</u> we can do to free ourselves. Just like in the slave-market, the only way to be set free is for the **ransom** to be paid.

HOW JESUS FREES US
We <u>all</u> sin. We all do what <u>we</u> want instead of what <u>God</u> wants. Our sin gets in the way between us and God. It stops us from knowing Him and stops us being His friends.

There's <u>nothing</u> we can do to free ourselves from sin. You can see why it's like being a slave!

Slave of sin

But when Jesus died on the cross, He was dying in our place, as our **ransom**—buying our freedom. <u>Jesus</u> paid the price for <u>our</u> sins.

When Jesus died, He dealt with the problem of sin. That means there is nothing to separate us from God any more. If we have put our trust in Jesus, then we have been freed from our sin. Instead of being slaves, we are free!

Freed by Jesus!

DAY 13
...and up he got!

KEYPOINT
Jesus has authority to forgive sins. He proves this by healing the paralysed man.

Today's passages are:
Table Talk: Mark 2v6-12
XTB: Mark 2v6-12

TABLE TALK

Use your model or picture of a Bible house to recap yesterday's story, ending with Jesus' words, "Your sins are forgiven."

READ

There were some religious leaders in the house, and they knew that only **God** can forgive sins. They 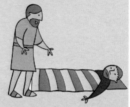 were horrified at Jesus' words! They think He is speaking *blasphemy* (lying about God). **Read Mark 2v6-12**

TALK

Jesus knew what the religious leaders were thinking—so He asked them a question. What was it? (v9) (*Is it easier to say "Your sins are forgiven" or to say "Get up and walk"?*)

THINK

Which one is easiest to **say**? (*It's easiest to say that someone's sins are forgiven, because no-one can see if it's come true or not!*) But Jesus **is** able to forgive sins. How did He prove it? (v10-12) (*He healed the man.*)

DO

Wow! Jesus proved that He has the authority to forgive sins. Add "Authority to forgive sins" to your Evidence Chart.

PRAY

If you have put your trust in Jesus, then your sins have been forgiven too! Thank Jesus for coming as your Rescuer to forgive your sins.

Building up
The people were all amazed (v12). If *you* had been there, which would you find the most amazing—Jesus' authority to heal the man, or His authority to forgive sins? Why?

DAY 14
The sin doctor

TABLE TALK

Imagine that Jesus is coming for dinner! Who else would you invite and why?

READ

In today's story, Jesus calls Levi to become one of his followers. Levi then invites Jesus home for dinner.
Read Mark 2v13-15

TALK

What was Levi's job? (v14) (*Tax collector*) What did that mean? (*Ask your child what they think, then fill in any gaps. In Jesus' time, tax collectors often stole from people, and they worked for the despised Romans. So everyone hated tax collectors!*) Who else was having dinner at Levi's house? (*Other tax collectors and sinners.*)

Jesus is know as "the friend of sinners". Why is this good news? (*Because <u>we</u> are sinners!*) Jesus came to forgive sins, so that people can be friends with God.

THINK

PRAY

Thank God that Jesus came to forgive sins. And even though we are sinners—He still wants to be our Friend.

Building up
Read Mark 2v16-17 The religious leaders were shocked that Jesus was spending time with 'bad' people. Read what Jesus said again. (See v17) What do you think He meant? (*People who think they're <u>well</u> don't go to the doctor!—just as people who are <u>proud</u> of themselves are unlikely to ask for forgiveness. It's people who know they are <u>sick</u> who go to the doctor. People like the tax collectors came to Jesus because they knew they <u>needed</u> forgiveness.*)

DAY 15
Fast food

Today's passages are:
Table Talk: Mark 2v18-20
XTB: Mark 2v18-20

TABLE TALK

My friend Jenny is seven. Last weekend she was bridesmaid at a wedding. She was very excited, and had a great time! Talk about any weddings you've been to. What did you enjoy most?

READ

In today's verses, Jesus says that He is like a **bridegroom**, and that His followers are like **guests** at a wedding. But first, we meet some people who are *fasting* (going without food for a while).
Read Mark 2v18-20

TALK

Who was fasting? (v18) (*John's followers and the Pharisees [religious leaders].*) Fasting was often a sign of <u>sorrow</u>. In those days many Jews fasted twice a week. They thought Jesus' disciples should fast as well, but what did Jesus say? (*Read v19 again.*)

THINK

If Jesus is the <u>bridegroom</u>, and His followers are the <u>guests</u>, then why don't they need to fast? (*It would be like being <u>sad</u> at a wedding!*) Weddings are times of great joy and happiness. Similarly, Jesus' coming is a time of great happiness. Why? (*He has come as our Rescuer, so that we can be forgiven and can be friends with God.*)

PRAY

Do you know any joyful songs about Jesus? If so, sing one together.

Building up
Read v20 again. What will happen later? (*Jesus will be taken from them, to die.*) At that time they will be full of sorrow. But their sorrow will turn to joy again! Why? (*Jesus came back to life again, and is still alive today!*)

DAY 16
New for old

Today's passages are:
Table Talk: Mark 2v21
XTB: Mark 2v21-22

TABLE TALK

Note: Your child may find this reading tricky to understand. To help them, copy these words into two speech bubbles:

 OLD — The Pharisees said, "You must keep our rules to please God."

 NEW — Jesus said, "Repent and believe the good news." (Mark 1v15)

DO

Collect two items of clothing (or pieces of cloth), one new and strong, the other old and worn. Compare the differences. I once patched old thin jeans with new strong denim—and the jeans tore round the edges of the patch! Why? (*The new denim was too strong for the old cloth.*)

READ

In today's verses Jesus is talking to the Pharisees. He shows them that their sets of rules are like <u>old</u> cloth—but that the great news about Jesus is <u>very different</u>!
Read Mark 2v21

What happens if you patch old clothes with new cloth? (v21) (*They rip.*)

THINK

Look at the two speech bubbles. If you try to fit Jesus' message into a human set of rules, it won't work! Why not? (*They're completely different. You can't become a Christian by keeping rules or trying to be good.*) That's great news since you can't be totally good all the time!

PRAY

Thank God that you don't need to keep a set of rules to be His friend. Thank Him for sending Jesus as your Rescuer.

Building up
Read v22. Same idea, different picture language. What happens if you pour raw new wine into old brittle wineskins? (v22) (*They'll split.*)

DAY 17
Corn on the job?

KEYPOINT
God's good rule gave the Sabbath as a day of **rest** —not a burden.

Today's passages are:
Table Talk: Mark 2v23-24, 27-28
XTB: Mark 2v23-28

TABLE TALK

In the Old Testament, God made a <u>good</u> rule. He said that one day a week—the Sabbath—was to be a day of **rest**. "*You shall do no work on the Sabbath.*" (Ex 20v10) But the Pharisees made lots of <u>extra</u> rules. They listed **39** things you mustn't do on the Sabbath! *Mime three of them* for your child to guess:

DO

• No walking (no more than 1 km from home)

• No reaping (no harvesting crops, like corn)

• No cooking (you prepared food the day before)

READ

Read Mark 2v23-24

Which of the Pharisees' rules did the disciples break? (*No reaping.*) The Pharisees thought this counted as work! But look at what Jesus told them:
Read Mark 2v27-28

TALK

What was the Sabbath made for? (v27) (*For people.*) God's good rule gave people a day of **rest**. But the Pharisees rules had turned it into a huge **burden**! Who is <u>Lord</u> of the Sabbath? (v28) (*The Son of Man—a title for Jesus.*) The Sabbath is **God's** day. But Jesus is in charge of it because He <u>is</u> God!

PRAY

Ask God to help you to spend your rest day pleasing Him, and enjoying the great things He has given us (including a rest from work and school!)

Building up
Today, most Christians have Sunday as their day of rest. It's a great day to meet with other Christians, to help people (as Jesus does in tomorrow's story) and to have a rest doing something you enjoy. Plan something to do together on your next rest day—and thank God for giving us a day of rest.

DAY 18
Hand it to him

KEYPOINT
It's always right to do **good** on the Sabbath.

Today's passages are:
Table Talk: Mark 3v1-5
XTB: Mark 3v1-6

TABLE TALK

Imagine one of you has cut your hand. Collect the things you would use to treat it. (*E.g. plasters, antiseptic...*) Would you treat it differently on a <u>Sunday</u>? (*No!*)

READ

Yesterday we saw that God made the Sabbath as a day of **rest**, but that the Pharisees filled it with lots of **rules** to keep. Today, there's another Sabbath argument. Should Jesus **_heal_** someone on the Sabbath or not?
Read Mark 3v1-5

TALK

The Pharisees said that you <u>could</u> heal someone on the Sabbath—but only if they were **dying**! Was this man dying? (v1) (*No!*) Did Jesus heal him? (v5) (*Yes!*)

THINK

Jesus could have waited until the next day to heal this man—but He didn't! Why not?—see v4. (*It's always right to do **good** on the Sabbath.*)

PRAY

Jesus <u>always</u> did what's good and right. Ask God to help you to be like Jesus—on every day of the week.

Building up
Look back at verse 2. Why were some people watching Jesus? (*To find a reason to get Him into trouble.*) Now read **verse 6** to see what the Pharisees did later. What Jesus did was **good** and **right**, but His enemies <u>hated</u> Him for it (and later had Him killed). If <u>you</u> do what's good and right, you might sometimes be hated or laughed at too. Ask God to help you to do the right thing. Pray that He'll help you to put up with any teasing you get.

DAY 19
Send in the crowds

KEYPOINT
Who is Jesus? An amazing healer? Or much more?

Today's passages are:
Table Talk: Mark 3v7-12
XTB: Mark 3v7-12

TABLE TALK

Flick through a paper or magazine for photos of famous people. If they came to your town would you go to see them? Why?

READ

Crowds flocked to see Jesus from far and wide. (*See map as you read the verses*).
Read Mark 3v7-12

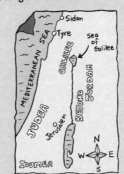

TALK

The crowds were pushing to get to Jesus, so what did He tell His disciples to do? (v9) (*Have a boat ready for Him.*) What did the crowds want? (v10) (*More healings.*) But Jesus was <u>much</u> more than just a healer! The evil spirits knew who Jesus was. Who? (v11) (*The Son of God.*) The evil spirits were right, but Jesus wouldn't let them tell the crowds. He knew the people wouldn't understand. They would follow Him for the wrong reasons.

THINK

The first half of Mark's book asks **"Who is Jesus?"**. How would you answer that question? (*A healer? The Son of God? Rescuer?...*)

PRAY

Who could you tell (or write to) about Jesus this week? Pray for them, and ask God to help you tell them about Jesus.

Building up
"Jesus was just a nice man. Nothing else." What could you say to someone who thinks this? Can you use some of the events in Mark's Gospel to explain who Jesus really is?

DAY 20
Follow the leader

KEYPOINT
Jesus chose twelve to be His apostles—"sent ones"—to spread the great news about Him.

Today's passages are:
Table Talk: Mark 3v13-19
XTB: Mark 3v13-19

DO

Write down as many of the Disciples' names as you can remember.
(*Pat yourselves on the back if you get 8; All take a bow if you get all 12!*)

READ

Tick off each name that you hear in the passage. **Read Mark 3v13-19**

TALK

Jesus had many followers, but He chose these twelve to be **Apostles**, which means "sent ones". What was He sending them to do? (v14-15) (*To preach the great news about Jesus, and to drive out evil spirits.*) From now on, Jesus spent a lot of time with these twelve. He was preparing them to tell others all about Him.

THINK

Think back over some of the things we've read about Jesus in Mark's book. (*Your Evidence Chart will help you.*) How would <u>you</u> feel if Jesus chose you to be one of His closest friends?

PRAY

The wonderful news is that Jesus <u>does</u> want you to be His friend! He loves you. He cares about you. He loves to listen to you pray. How does that make you feel? Talk to Jesus about it now.

Building up
Compare **Mark 3v6** with **3v19**. How are they linked? (*Judas betrayed Jesus to His enemies, so that they could kill Him.*) The rest of Mark's Gospel shows this wicked plot coming true—but amazingly it's all part of <u>God's</u> plan! Jesus loves us so much, that He came to die for us, so that we can be His friends for ever! Praise and thank Him now.

Notes for Parents

Counting up

THE BOOK OF NUMBERS

Numbers continues the story of the Israelites. It's a story that started in Genesis...

KEYPOINT
God kept His promise to give Abraham a huge family. There were over two million of them!

Today's passages are:
Table Talk: Numbers 1v1-3 & 46
XTB: Numbers 1v1-4 & 46

GENESIS

In the book of **Genesis**, God made three amazing promises to Abraham.

1 LAND → God promised to give Abraham's family the land of Canaan to live in.

2 CHILDREN → God said that Abraham's family would be so HUGE that there would be too many to count!

3 BLESSING → God promised that someone from Abraham's family would be God's way of blessing the whole world.

EXODUS

700 years later, Abraham's family were known as the *Israelites*. The book of **Exodus** tells us how they were rescued from Egypt (where they were slaves) and started on their journey to the promised land of Canaan.

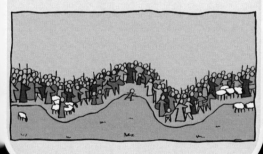

NUMBERS

In this issue of Table Talk we're going to be reading the book of **Numbers**. It tells us what happened to the Israelites on their journey to the promised land of Canaan.

TABLE TALK

Find out about the Book of Numbers in **Notes for Parents**.

How many of you are there? Now find different ways to count yourselves. E.g. How many children? How many wearing something red? How many males?

READ

At the beginning of Numbers, Moses holds a **census**—to <u>count</u> the Israelites. But he doesn't count all of them...
Read Numbers 1v1-3

TALK

Moses didn't count the <u>children</u>, or the <u>women</u>. Who did he count? (v2-3) (*All the men who were 20+ and could fight in the army.*) Chapter One has a long list of the people who helped Moses to do the counting. At the end we find the grand total. How many men were there? (See **v46**, which in some Bibles is at the end of a table of numbers.) (*603,550*)

That's a HUGE number. But who <u>didn't</u> they count? (*Women and children.*)
If you add women and children as well there were probably more than ***Two Million Israelites!!***

God had kept His promise to Abraham, and given him a HUGE family. Thank God that He <u>always</u> keeps His promises.

PRAY

Building up

Look back at God's original promise to Abraham in **Genesis 15v5-6**. Did Abraham (called Abram here) believe God? (v6) (Yes) Abraham was right to believe God. By the time of Numbers, there were more than two million men, women and children in his family!

DAY 22
Lorryloads of Levis

Today's passages are:
Table Talk: Numbers 1v47-50 & 54
XTB: Numbers 1v47-54

TABLE TALK

The Israelites were divided into twelve **tribes**. Each was the family of one of Jacob's twelve sons. Look at the picture and spot whose family the **Levites** are. (*The descendants of Levi.*)

Do you know any other Levi's? (*Jesus had a disciple called Levi—Mark 2v14; Levi Strauss invented riveted jeans in 1873!*)

READ

When Moses counted up all the Israelites, he <u>didn't</u> count the Levites.
Read Numbers 1v47-50

TALK

Yesterday, we read that Moses counted all the men who could do what? (*Fight in the army.*) He <u>didn't</u> count the Levites—they had a different job to do. What was it? (v50) (*They were in charge of the tabernacle/tent of God's presence.*)
More about this tabernacle (tent) tomorrow.

READ

What do we learn about the Israelites in **v54**? (*They did everything God said.*)

PRAY

Sadly, the Israelites <u>didn't</u> always obey God (as we'll see later). But this time they did exactly what He said. Ask God to help <u>you</u> to live His way, too.

Building up
Read the story of Moses' birth in **Exodus 2v1-4**. Which tribe was Moses from? (v1) (*Levi*) Moses, his brother Aaron, and his sister Miriam, were all Levites. Although the Levites all had responsibilities for the tabernacle, it was only <u>Aaron's</u> family who became priests (Exodus 29v5-9).

DAY 23
God is with us

Today's passages are:
Table Talk: Exodus 25v1-9
XTB: Exodus 25v1-9

Imagine that you are going to make a tent. What would you make it from? (*E.g. fabric, poles, rope...*)

READ

Back in Exodus, God had told the Israelites to make a kind of tent. It was called the **tabernacle**. First, they collected things to make it from. Listen to what they collected. Are there any surprises? **Read Exodus 25v1-9**

TALK

What surprising things did they make the tabernacle from? (*E.g. gold, silver, bronze; hides of sea cows; gem stones.*) This was obviously a very special tent! Find out more about it in **Notes for Parents** on the next page.

THINK

Read **verse 2** again. Only people who really **wanted** to give to God's work did so. Are <u>you</u> like that? Are you happy to give to God? Talk about the things you can give Him. (*E.g. your time [maybe to help someone, or tell others about Him], your money, your abilities...*)

PRAY

Pray together about your answers.

Building up
Later in Exodus, we find out that the Israelites gave so generously that Moses had to stop them! **Read Exodus 36v3-7** Do you want to give to God that generously? Pray about your answers.

Notes for Parents

THE TABERNACLE

The **tabernacle** was a tent. It looked like this:

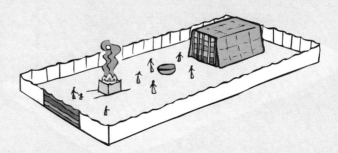

The Israelites moved around a lot. So the tabernacle was designed to be easily taken apart. They could pack it up, pick it up and take it with them. Wherever they stopped, the Israelites camped in their tribes round the four sides of the tabernacle. It was in the centre, reminding them that **God was with them all the time**.

THE ARK OF THE COVENANT (THE COVENANT BOX)

The ark was a wooden box, covered in gold. It was carried on two wooden poles, also covered in gold.

When God gave the Ten Commandments to Moses, He wrote them on two stone tablets. These are called the **testimony**. They were kept in the <u>ark</u>, which was inside the <u>tabernacle</u>. For this reason, the tabernacle is sometimes called the **Tent of the Testimony**.

THE ATONEMENT COVER (THE MERCY SEAT)

The lid of the ark had two gold cherubim (angels) on it.

The lid was like a throne for God. He said that He would meet with His people there.

But there was a problem! God is perfect and pure. But the Israelites were sinful (disobedient) people. Their sin got in the way between them and God. They <u>couldn't</u> just meet with Him!

The only way the people could be with God was if He showed them **mercy** (undeserved kindness) and forgave their sins. This is called **atonement**.

That's why this lid was called the **mercy seat** or **atonement cover**.

DAY 24
Ark lark

TABLE TALK

Play **hangman** to guess the phrase "The Ark of the Covenant".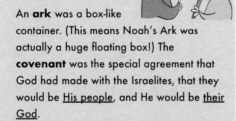

An **ark** was a box-like container. (This means Noah's Ark was actually a huge floating box!) The **covenant** was the special agreement that God had made with the Israelites, that they would be <u>His people</u>, and He would be <u>their God</u>.

READ

The ark (sometimes called the Covenant Box) was kept inside the tabernacle. **Read Exodus 25v10-16**

TALK

What was the ark made of? (v10) (Acacia wood.) What was it covered with? (v11) (Gold) The ark was carried on two poles. See the picture in **Notes for Parents** opposite.

What was kept <u>inside</u> the ark? (v16) (The testimony/stone tablets with the ten commandments on them.)

THINK

The two stone tablets held God's special commands to His people. So they were kept safe in this golden ark, like the most valuable treasure. Are God's words <u>special</u> to you? If so, should you keep your Bible in a gold box? (No!) How can you show that God's words are special to you? (By reading the Bible and doing what it says.)

Ask God to help you to do that.

PRAY

Building up
Find out more about the ark in **Notes for Parents**.

DAY 25
Keep a lid on it

TABLE TALK

Yesterday we read about the ark. This special box had a special lid. Look at the picture of it in **Notes for Parents**. What was on top of the lid? (Two cherubim/angels.)

READ

Read Exodus 25v21-22

This lid was like a throne for God. What did God say He would do there? (v22) (Meet with them, and give them His laws.)

But the Israelites <u>couldn't</u> just meet with God! They were sinful (disobedient) people, and their sin got in the way between them and God. For this reason, the lid has two special names. It is sometimes called the **atonement cover** or the **mercy seat**. Find out more in **Notes for Parents**.

THINK

Like those Israelites, we <u>all</u> sin. And our sin stops us from being with God. But God showed us **mercy**. He sent Jesus to die on the cross to take the punishment for our sins. Jesus paid the price (**atoned**) for our sins, so that we can be forgiven.

PRAY

Thank God for sending Jesus to die in your place so that you can be forgiven.

Building up
The book of Hebrews picks up the picture of approaching God's throne through His **mercy**. **Read Hebrews 4v14-16** Who is our great High Priest? (v14) (Jesus) It is because of <u>Jesus</u> that we can come to God. Praise and thank Him!

DAY 26
Follow that cloud

Today's passages are:
Table Talk: Numbers 9v15-18
XTB: Numbers 9v15-23

TABLE TALK

Talk about any school trips or church outings you've been on. How do your teachers/leaders make sure everyone knows where to go and no-one gets lost?

READ

Now that we've found out about the ark and the tabernacle, it's time to get back to the book of **Numbers**—where something has settled over the tabernacle.
Read Numbers 9v15-18

TALK

What was over the tabernacle? (v15) (A cloud.) If the cloud **lifted** from the tabernacle, what must the Israelites do? (v17) (Set out on their journey.) If the cloud **settled**, what must they do? (v17) (Make camp.)

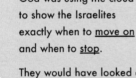

God was using the cloud to show the Israelites exactly when to <u>move on</u> and when to <u>stop</u>.

THINK

They would have looked at that cloud every day to check what God wanted them to do. They wouldn't want to miss His instructions! How about <u>you</u>? How does God show you what He wants you to do? (In the Bible.)

PRAY

How often do you read your Bible, and how carefully do you follow God's instructions? Talk to Him about your answers.

Building up

God had already used this cloud to lead the Israelites when He rescued them from Egypt. Read about it in **Exodus 13v21-22**. God had already led the Israelites safely across the Red Sea. Now He would guide them safely across the desert to the promised land of Canaan.

DAY 27
Trumpet calls

Today's passages are:
Table Talk: Numbers 10v1-4
XTB: Numbers 10v1-10

TABLE TALK

Take it in turns to imitate sounds designed to get our attention. Ask the others to guess what they are. E.g. doorbell, telephone, police siren, school bell, alarm clock...

READ

Do you remember how many Israelites there were? (Over two million!—Day 21) It would be hard to get the attention of that many people. So God told Moses to make something to help.
Read Numbers 10v1-4

TALK

What did Moses make? (v2) (Two silver trumpets.) What were some of the reasons for using them? (v2—to tell the people to set out; v3—to call everyone together; v4—call the leaders together.)

READ

Look back to **Numbers 9v23**, and ahead to **Numbers 10v13**. Did the Israelites obey God's instructions? (Yes)

PRAY

When your alarm clock goes off, how quickly do you get up? Do you just turn over and go back to sleep?!! Ask God to help you <u>not</u> to be like that with Him! Ask Him to help you to obey Him quickly and willingly.

Building up

Read Numbers 10v5-10 Did you notice the echo of a promise in verse 9? Look back to the three promises in **Notes for Parents** on Day 21. Which promise is God mentioning here? (A land of their own.) God <u>did</u> keep His promise to bring the Israelites to the land of Canaan. (You can read about it in Joshua 1v1-6.) Thank God for always keeping His promises.

DAY 28
Goodbye to Sinai

KEYPOINT
The Israelites set off on their journey to the promised land, following God's command.

Today's passages are:
Table Talk: Numbers 10v11-13 & 33
XTB: Numbers 10v11-36

 TABLE TALK

 Imagine you're going on holiday tomorrow. Each name three things you would take with you.

READ The Israelites have been camped at Mount Sinai for nearly a year. But now it's time to set off. They're not going on holiday! It's time to go to the land God has promised them. **Read Numbers 10v11-13**

TALK How did the Israelites know it was time to go? (v11) (*The cloud lifted from the tabernacle.*) Whose command were they following? (v13) (*The LORD's.*)

This first part of the journey lasted for three days. **Read verse 33**. What went ahead of the Israelites? (*The ark.*)

This was a sign that <u>God</u> was with them.

THINK Imagine you were one of the Israelites, setting off on your journey to the promised land. How would you feel?

PRAY God had promised that He would bring the Israelites to Canaan, but they still had to <u>trust</u> Him to do it. Do you sometimes worry about the future? Talk to God about anything you're worried about. Ask Him to help you to trust Him.

Building up
Read Numbers 10v29-32. Moses invited his brother-in-law, Hobab, to come with them. What did Moses clearly believe about God? (v29 & 32) (*That God would keep His promises to them.*) Why do you think Moses was so sure? (*Think back to what you know about Moses and the things he had seen God do.*)

DAY 29
Roaming and moaning

KEYPOINT
God was angry with the Israelites because they were complaining.

Today's passages are:
Table Talk: Numbers 11v1-3
XTB: Numbers 11v1-3

 TABLE TALK

Draw a happy face. Round it write or draw some of the great things God had done for the Israelites. (*E.g. rescued them from Egypt; given them the ten commandments; promised to be with them; given them a cloud to follow to show them the way to Canaan.*)

READ How should the Israelites <u>feel</u>? (*Thankful to their great God.*) But now ***draw a grumpy face***. Instead of being thankful, the Israelites started to moan... **Read Numbers 11v1-3**

TALK Who heard the Israelites moaning? (v1) (*God*) God was <u>angry</u> at their complaining. What did He do? (v1) (*Sent fire to the Israelite camp.*) Moses needed to ask God to forgive the Israelites. What happened then? (v2) (*The fire died down.*)

THINK Would you be ashamed of moaning if you remembered that **God** is listening? God gives us everything we have—our food, our homes, our friends, our possessions—EVERYTHING! But often, instead of saying thank you, we just moan about them!

PRAY Think of some ways <u>you've</u> been moaning recently. Say sorry to God and ask Him to help you not to be a moaner.

Building up
Read Philippians 4v4-7. Notice how very different this is from the attitude of the Israelites! Is it easy to be this kind of person? Ask God to help you!

DAY 30
Mind your mannas

KEYPOINT
Instead of being grateful, the Israelites complained about the manna God gave them to eat.

Today's passages are:
Table Talk: Numbers 11v4-6 & 10
XTB: Numbers 11v4-10

TABLE TALK

The Israelites were travelling across the desert. That's a hard place to find food. Do you remember how God was feeding them? (*Every morning, they gathered white flakes that had settled on the ground. This food was called* **manna**. *It tasted like biscuits made with honey.*)

READ

Manna was God's good gift to the Israelites. It kept them alive and healthy. But look how they felt about it...
Read Numbers 11v4-6

TALK

Were the Israelites grateful? (*No!*) What did they remember eating in Egypt? (*See v5.*) Of course, they were forgetting that they had been <u>slaves</u> in Egypt!
Read how God felt about their moaning.
Read verse 10.

How did God feel? (*He was angry.*) More about God's reaction tomorrow.

THINK

<u>Our</u> food doesn't settle on the ground overnight! Where does it come from? (*E.g. shops, farms, your own garden...*) But the Bible says that <u>everything</u> we have comes from God. That includes our food.

PRAY

Thank God for the food that He gives you—and also for the people who cook it. (Say a big thank-you to them today!)

Building up
Find out more about manna in **Numbers 11v7-9** and also **Exodus 16v31-36**.

DAY 31
More moaning

KEYPOINT
Moses moaned too—but God was kind to him, and gave him 70 leaders to help him.

Today's passages are:
Table Talk: Numbers 11v16-17
XTB: Numbers 11v10-17

TABLE TALK

Every Israelite family was moaning at the same time! Mimic the sound they made by all speaking at once, saying things like: "It's not fair!", "We want meat!", "Manna is boring!", "It was better in Egypt!"

THINK

How do you think Moses felt as he heard them all moaning?

Moses started moaning too. "Why have you brought this trouble on me?", he asked God. "It's all too much for me!"

READ

How do you think God will respond? Read the verses to find out.
Read Numbers 11v16-17

TALK

Even though Moses was grumbling at God, God was **kind** to him. What did he give Moses to help him? (*70 leaders.*) These leaders would help Moses, so that he didn't have to do everything himself.

THINK

Did you know that you can be completely honest with God? If you're worried, upset or fed up—you can tell Him! Moaning is never right (as we saw on Day 29), but we can always tell God the <u>truth</u> about how we feel.

PRAY

Talk to God now about how you're feeling (good as well as bad), and thank Him that you can be completely honest with Him.

Building up
Read Psalm 139v1-4. God knows all our thoughts and feelings, so there's no point hiding them from Him. Be totally honest with Him, and ask for any help you need. If there are attitudes that need to change, ask Him to help with those too—see **Psalm 139v23-24**.

DAY 32
Mission impossible?

KEYPOINT
Nothing is impossible for God.

Today's passages are:
Table Talk: Numbers 11v19-23
XTB: Numbers 11v18-23

DO

Make a poster with these verses on it.

"Nothing is impossible with God."
Luke 1v37

"With God all things are possible."
Matthew 19v26

READ

The Israelites have been grumbling about eating **manna** all the time. They want **meat**. Now God says He will give them meat—loads of it!
Read Numbers 11v19-23

TALK

How long was God going to give them meat for? (v20) (*A month.*) Will they be grateful? (v20) (*No! They'll end up loathing it!*) But what was Moses worried about? (v21-22) (*Where all the meat would come from.*)

THINK

God's reply reminded Moses of His power. "Is the Lord's arm too short?", God asked. (v23, NIV) A **short arm** wouldn't be able to do much! But is God like that? (*No!*) Moses and the Israelites will soon see where all the meat will come from.

PRAY

Read the words on your poster again. Thank God that nothing is impossible for Him.

Building up
Find out more about the words on your poster by reading **Luke 1v30-38** and **Matthew 19v23-26**. God was able to make Mary pregnant, so that she would be the mother of His Son, Jesus. And He is able to bring sinful people like you and me to know and love Jesus. Thank God for these things!

DAY 33
Holy helper

KEYPOINT
In the Old T, God gave His Spirit to selected people. Now He gives the Spirit to all believers.

Today's passages are:
Table Talk: Numbers 11v24-25 & 29-30
XTB: Numbers 11v24-30

TABLE TALK

Play **hangman** to guess "The Holy Spirit". What do you know about the Holy Spirit? (*He isn't a force—like electricity! He's a person. He's God.*)

READ

Do you remember God's promise to give Moses some men to help him lead the Israelites? How many did He give? (*Day 31—70 leaders.*) Moses already had God's Holy Spirit. These 70 men would need the Spirit too, to help them serve God. **Read Numbers 11v24-25**

TALK

What happened when the 70 men were given God's Spirit? (v25) (*They began to **prophesy**—to speak God's message.*) But two men weren't prophesying in the same place as the others. So Joshua wanted to stop them.
Read Numbers 11v29-30

What did Moses say he wished God would do? (v29) (*Give Spirit to all His people.*)

THINK

In the Old Testament, God gave His Spirit to selected people who had special jobs. (*There are examples in **Building Up** below.*) But in the New Testament, God gives the Holy Spirit to **all** believers.

PRAY

If you are a Christian, God has given you His Spirit too, to help you to serve God and live His way. Thank God for the amazing gift of His Spirit to help you live for Him.

Building up
Read about three examples of God giving His Spirit to selected people in the Old Testament, to help them with special jobs. Read about Bezalel (Exodus 31v1-5), Gideon (Judges 6v34) and Samson (Judges 14v5-6).

Sitting and walking :
A PARENTS GUIDE

These commandments that I give you today are to be upon your hearts. Impress them on your children. Talk about them when you sit at home and when you walk along the road, when you lie down and when you get up. Tie them as symbols on your hands and bind them on your foreheads. Write them on the doorframes of your houses and on your gates.

When the LORD your God brings you into the land he swore to your fathers, to Abraham, Isaac and Jacob, to give you—a land with large, flourishing cities you did not build, houses filled with all kinds of good things you did not provide, wells you did not dig, and vineyards and olive groves you did not plant — then when you eat and are satisfied, be careful that you do not forget the LORD, who brought you out of Egypt, out of the land of slavery.

Deuteronomy 6 v 6-12

The main reason we decided to publish *Table Talk* was because we started to discover how little help there was around for parents in teaching God's word and the Christian way to children. Furtive discussions with other Dads and Mums revealed that we were not alone in feeling that we were complete failures in this area. If the Christian influence we give to our children is confined to Church (Sunday School—taught by someone else!) and the occasional Bible story and bedtime prayer, then our kids will soon get the message that we are pretty half-hearted about the whole thing.

It may be that we have fallen into the trap that Moses warned the People of God about in this passage. Now that we are enjoying all the benefits of living in a comfortable environment, supportive church family, enjoyable life style etc. the plain realities of the world as God sees it can grow faint. Just as the Israelites forgot how the Lord had saved them from Egypt when they were living in the promised land, so we

can become blunt and unfocussed in our witness to our children.

It's why Moses encourages them, not just to go to the synagogue week by week, but to surround themselves with reminders of all that God has done for us. Not just when you lie down (v7) but when you are sitting around and travelling. And not just <u>talking</u> about things, but having <u>physical</u> reminders around the house. In their case this meant wearing physical symbols, and marking the doors of their houses. Today, we might wear badges or crosses, or put texts on the wall or on the fridge.

Here are some ideas for how you can appropriately make talking about God more a part of the fabric of daily family life, rather than a weekend and night-time 'bolt on' option.

... when you sit at home...

Most families will spend a considerable amount of sitting around time in front of what an earlier generation of Christians called 'The Haunted Fish Tank'—the telly! TV is a powerful medium, and the danger for us is that we tend to be passive in front of it. That is, we relax and

enjoy the story. It takes an effort to kick into gear and start to discuss issues that are raised by a programme.

Younger children are very black and white about moral issues—often asking us to identify which is the 'goody' and which is the 'baddy'. Some simple questions at the end of the film can have a good influence on your child's ability to relate the story to God's bigger picture. Questions like:

• What did you enjoy about that?
• Who did you like best in it? Why?
• Why do you think she did that?

- Who would you most like to be in that film?
- What do you think God feels about that bad man/woman/chipmunk?

These kinds of questions give you the opportunity to talk about how God is saddened by sin; issues of justice and judgement; love and faithfulness. It is remarkable too how many film plots are built around themes of love and self sacrifice which will present an opportunity to point to God's love for us and the sacrifice of Jesus for our sins. But remember, the Gospel is always 'stranger than fiction', in that Christ died for us while we were still enemies. (See Romans 5 v7-8—would the 'hero' have risked himself for the baddy?)

There are increasing opportunities once children have started to reach the age of 8 or so to start discussing moral ambiguity and motivation of people in films and TV programmes. *Warning: sometimes kids just want to enjoy the film—not have a 20-minute discussion about it afterwards!*

Having a few Christian or Bible-based videos is useful, but it is ultimately unhelpful if we limit our children's viewing to these. They need to relate to our fallen world, and to learn how to see the world through the Word.

... when you walk along the road...

I am able to walk two of my children to school each morning, and (if we're not late and rushing) this has proven to be one of the most fruitful opportunities for talking about the Lord with them. Whether it's commenting on the trees, plants or seasons (wasn't God brilliant in the way He made that...), talking over things learned at school, or people they know, there is always room for making God part of the picture.

When I praise my children for the things that they are especially good at (Jenny: art; Maggie: stories; Lizzie: hand-to-hand combat) I always try to remind them that these abilities are from God the most generous gift giver, who delights in giving different things to different people. This will hopefully help them to appreciate others as well as to be humble about their own abilities.

Having a CD or tape of Christian sing-along songs in the car can help break up a tedious journey, and there are also some decent story tapes available retelling Bible stories in fun and imaginative ways.

... when you lie down and when you get up...

Bedtime is an appropriate time for prayers (see *Miracles and Dreams Table Talk*), or for doing some child-based Bible notes (like *XTB* or *Discover*) and stories; Morning is our best time for doing *Table Talk*—but even if it's not appropriate, then taking the trouble to say a prayer for the day at breakfast can be a helpful discipline to get into.

Needless to say there is always the danger of 'hothousing' your children in a spiritually unhelpful way. And often we should take the lead from them, and give them the space to ask questions which we can respond to.

And their questions can be rather wonderful. I was staring out the window with my three girls one evening looking at some wonderful cloud shapes. "You know, one day, the Lord Jesus will be coming back on the clouds in great glory, and will take us to be with Him in Heaven," I said. There was a pause while the girls took this in, and then Jenny asked: "Will we have time to put our shoes on?"

Tim Thornborough

> I am able to walk two of my children to school each morning, and (if we're not late and rushing) this has proven to be one of the most fruitful opportunities for talking about the Lord with them.

DAY 34
Three fab facts

KEYPOINT
God keeps His word.
God is powerful.
God punishes sin.

Today's passages are:
Table Talk: Numbers 11v31-35
XTB: Numbers 11v31-35

TABLE TALK

Write out these three sentences on some paper: God keeps His word. God is powerful. God punishes sin.

READ

What had the Israelites been moaning about? (*Eating manna when they wanted meat.*) Find out what happened next.
Read Numbers 11v31-35

TALK

Look at your three sentences again:

God keeps His word. What promise does God keep? (*To give meat.*)

God is powerful. How does God show His power? (v31) (*By sending huge numbers of quail.*)

God punishes sin. The Israelites <u>sinned</u> when they moaned about God's good gift of manna. How does God punish them? (v33) (*With a plague.*)

THINK

These three facts are all still true. God is just as *powerful* today. (As we saw on Day 32, <u>nothing</u> is impossible for God.) And He still *punishes* sin. But long before the time of Moses, God had made a promise to send a <u>Rescuer</u>, to save His people. God's Rescuer would take the punishment for our sin, so that we can be forgiven. God kept His *word*, and sent that Rescuer. Who did He send? (*Jesus*)

PRAY

Thank God for keeping His word to send Jesus as our Rescuer, to save those who believe in Him.

Building up
Read Jesus' own summary of this in **John 3v16-18**. Praise Jesus for coming as your Rescuer.

DAY 35
Moanalots!

KEYPOINT
Unlike the Israelites, we should be thankful for all that God has done for us.

Today's passages are:
Table Talk: 1 Thessalonians 5v16-18
XTB: 1 Thessalonians 5v16-18

TABLE TALK

Take it in turns to say this phrase with a grumbling, moaning voice: "Do I <u>have</u> to wash up? I did it yesterday!" Whose voice had the most believable whine in it??

READ

It's fun to put on a pretend moaning voice. But the sad truth is that many of us really are *moanalots*! But read what Paul says we should actually be like. It's from his letter to Christians in Thessalonica, in Greece. **Read 1 Thessalonians 5v16-18**

TALK

What are the three things Paul says we should do? (*Be joyful, prayerful and thankful.*)

THINK

What do you think it means to be thankful in all circumstances? (*Give thanks all the time, no matter how things are.*) Do you think that's easy? What might help you? (*E.g. encourage each other to keep thanking God, even in hard times; make a list of reasons to thank Him...*)

PRAY

Think of some things now that you can thank God for. Then thank Him for each one—and ask Him to help you not to be a moanalot!

Building up
Psalm 136 lists many reasons why the Israelites should have been thankful to God. ***Read it***. This psalm was written long ago, but the chorus remains true—God's love <u>is</u> eternal, it endures for ever. Praise and thank Him for His everlasting love.

Notes for Parents

1, 2, 3, Go!

EXPLORING EPHESIANS

Over the next 15 days, we are taking a look at Paul's letter to the Christians in Ephesus. When we write letters today, they tend to be much shorter than this one. In Paul's time, there were no telephones, or email and even the transport was very different from today. It is probably true to say that letters were sent less often, but were longer. They would have been delivered by hand and taken a long time to arrive.

When Paul wrote a letter to his friends or a specific church, he always had a purpose in mind. It may have been to:

- Encourage them

- Put them right about something

- Discipline them (correct and train them)

- Warn them

- Teach them something specific about Jesus or God

- Remind them about something important

His letters often included several of these.

Paul's letter to the **Ephesians** contains many very big ideas, which could get you a bit 'bogged' down. It is very important that you concentrate on some of the overall themes of the letter, rather than every bit of detail. Don't be distracted.

In this series we are going to look at the first half of Ephesians, chapters 1-3. They help us to see the importance of unity in the church through what Jesus has done on the cross. Paul explains what God has done through Jesus in bringing together Jews and Gentiles (non-Jews) in His church, for His praise and glory.

EPHESUS FACT FILE

This city was the most important one in the region (now known as Turkey). It was a harbour and the centre of the major, thriving, trade route. The city was made up of a diverse group of people from all over the region.

Look at an atlas and find Izmir (Smyrna) in Turkey. The ruins of Ephesus are near here.

KEYPOINT
Paul wants to tell others about what Jesus has given to those who believe in Him.

Today's passages are:
Table Talk: Ephesians 1v1-3
XTB: Ephesians 1v1-3

TABLE TALK

What kinds of post can you get? (*Letters, postcards, parcels, bills, leaflets.*) How does it feel when you get post? Over the next 15 days we are looking at a letter written by Paul to a church at Ephesus. (See **Notes for Parents** to find out about it.)

READ

When you write a letter to someone, how do you <u>start</u> it? How do you <u>end</u> it? Paul's letter is a little different.
Read Ephesians 1v1-3

TALK

How was Paul's letter different? (v1) (*Starts with who it is from; addressed to God's people.*) Your Bible may say 'Saints' in v1. This means everyone who believes and trusts in Jesus. Why did Paul write letters to God's people? (*Check out some reasons in Notes for Parents.*)

THINK

What are some reasons why <u>you</u> write letters? (*Encourage someone, remind them of something, thank them...*) Paul was so excited about God's kindness in what Jesus had done, that he had to write about it! What does Paul say God has given us? (v3) (*Every spiritual blessing— that's the good things God gives us because of Jesus.*) We'll find out more about exactly what those blessings are in the next few days.

PRAY

Dear God, thank you for loving us so much and sending Jesus so we can be in your family. Help us to tell others about you. Amen

Building up
Read the *Ephesus Fact File* in **Notes for Parents** to find out more about Ephesus.

DAY 37
Chosen children

KEYPOINT
God chose us to be His followers, before we were even born.

Today's passages are:
Table Talk: Ephesians 1v4-6
XTB: Ephesians 1v4-6

TABLE TALK

If you could choose <u>anyone</u> to be your best friend, who would you choose? (It could be someone famous.) Why would you choose them? Draw a picture of them (or cut one out and stick it). Around the picture, write why you would choose them. (*Keep this for Day 41.*)

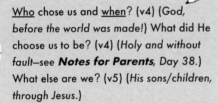

READ

Read Ephesians 1v4-6

<u>Who</u> chose us and <u>when</u>? (v4) (*God, before the world was made!*) What did He choose us to be? (v4) (*Holy and without fault—see* **Notes for Parents***, Day 38.*) What else are we? (v5) (*His sons/children, through Jesus.*)

TALK

THINK

Spend a minute thinking about your friends and why they are your friends. Is it because they are nice, good, kind, friendly, clever, or for other reasons?

God has NOT chosen us because we are really nice or good—but because He WANTED to!

Being God's children is one of the amazing spiritual blessings we have because of Jesus.

PRAY

Dear God, you're wonderful. You've given us every spiritual blessing because of Jesus. Thank you. Amen

Building up
How do we know that God has chosen us?— because we believe in Jesus. **Read John 1v12-13.** Have <u>you</u> been chosen by God to be one of His children? (*If you have put your trust in Jesus—you have!*)

GREAT NEW WORDS
As you work through Ephesians together, you will come across some Great New Words. Below is an explanation for each, together with a symbol to help you. Understanding these words will be a big help in getting to grips with God and His great plan.

GRACE
- When God gives us what we <u>don't</u> deserve.
- Grace is God's HUGE kindness to people who don't deserve it.
- An undeserved gift. (*Throughout Days 36-50*)

MERCY
- When God does <u>not</u> give us what we deserve.
- God's decision to help us and not treat us the way we deserve. (*Day 44*)

SALVATION
- To be saved, by Jesus, through His death and resurrection. (*Throughout Days 36-50*)

HOLY (and BLAMELESS) 100%
- To be seen as special in God's eyes, perfect and as if you had NEVER done anything wrong. (*Day 37*)

REDEEM / REDEMPTION
- The price to pay for someone's freedom or rescue.
- To pay for something, which used to belong to you, so you can own it again. (*Day 38*)

GOSPEL
- The good news about Jesus and what He has done. (*Day 40*)

RECONCILE
- To bring people back together again.
- To mend a relationship, which has been broken. (*Day 45*)

REVELATION / REVEAL
- To make sense of something.
- For God to make something understood, about Himself. (*Day 41*)

DAY 38
Free and forgiven

KEYPOINT
Jesus' death on the cross was the payment needed to give us freedom and forgiveness.

Today's passages are:
Table Talk: Ephesians 1v7-8
XTB: Ephesians 1v7-8

TABLE TALK

DO

Get two pieces of string three feet long with loops at each end. One piece for each person. Put your hands through the loops (like handcuffs) but make sure your string comes between your partners string and his/her body so that you're connected. Now get separated without a) taking the string off or b) breaking the string!

Explain that being tied together is like being a <u>slave</u>. Being set <u>free</u> can only happen if you have the answer.

Answer: Take your piece of string <u>through</u> your partner's **loop** and <u>over</u> his/her **wrist**.

READ

The answer to the game was quite easy. But God says we are <u>trapped</u> by sin so that we are <u>separated</u> from God. This is like being a **slave**. **Read Ephesians 1v7-8** to see how we can be set free.

TALK

Use **Notes for Parents** to check the meaning of another great word— **Redemption**. What was the price for us to be set free? (v7) (*Jesus' sacrificial death— this means His death on the cross*). Just like the game, <u>we</u> can't work out how to get free of sin. We <u>can't</u> free ourselves. But **God** has done it for us.

PRAY

Paul loves to <u>praise</u> God for the things He has done. It's a good pattern to follow, so praise God for Jesus dying on the cross and giving us freedom and forgiveness.

Building up
Think about the difference between being a <u>slave</u> and being <u>free</u>. Make a list of these differences. Which is the best way to live?

DAY 39
A grand plan

KEYPOINT
God's rescue plan will eventually result in a whole new world with Jesus in charge.

Today's passages are:
Table Talk: Ephesians 1v9-10
XTB: Ephesians 1v9-10

TABLE TALK

Draw a treasure map and put a cross (X) where the treasure is buried. (*Keep it for later.*) If it was a real map you wouldn't find the treasure until you found the X. The map becomes the secret plan.

READ

In our passage today we can see another plan, which involves a mystery and a fantastic end result. To get to that end result involves a cross as well. **Read Ephesians 1v9-10**

THINK

God wants you to <u>know</u> His secret plan! It <u>will</u> be completed because God has dealt with sin already. How did He do it?

(*Solve the mystery*)

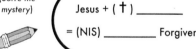
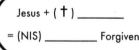

Jesus + (†) _____
= (NIS) _____ Forgiven

The final plan will come true in the future, when God makes a new world, where **no sin** will exist! Who will be in charge at the centre of everything? (*v10—Jesus*)

DO

On the bottom of your treasure map write, "God's plans always happen!"

PRAY

Thank you Father that your plans always come true. Thank you that one day Jesus will be in charge of everyone and everything in a perfect world. Amen.

Building up
The worst thing about a mystery or secret plan is not being able to work it out. But God's Secret plan <u>isn't</u> a mystery. **Read Ephesians 1 v 10 again** to remind yourself what it is.

DAY 40
It's for you

KEYPOINT
God keeps His promises, and to prove it He's given His Holy Spirit to those who believe in Jesus.

Today's passages are:
Table Talk: Ephesians 1v13-14
XTB: Ephesians 1v11-14

(You need paper, pencil, a candle, matches and a small coin, e.g. 5p.) Write a short letter, making a promise to do something (e.g. help make your bed, wash the car). Melt some candle wax onto the bottom of the letter and push the coin into it before it goes hard. Then remove the coin.

This is called **sealing** a letter and it confirms that what is said will happen. In the past, families had their own seal so others would know who had made the promise. It was a stamp of ownership.

Our passage today talks about God's promise and His stamp of ownership—His seal. **Read Ephesians 1v13-14**

Who did we hear about saving us? (v13) (Jesus) What kind of news is this? (v13) (Good news. Some Bibles use the word "Gospel"—which means Good News.) Having believed, what was given? (v13) (The Holy Spirit.) He is a stamp of ownership/seal, to make sure we know God will keep His promises.

Having God's stamp of ownership in your life, the Holy Spirit, is the best thing in the world. If you are a Christian thank God for giving you His Holy Spirit to help you and to guarantee His promises.

Building up
Can you think of any promises God has made in the Bible? Try looking up some of these:
John1v12; John 3v15; Hebrews 13v5.
What's the difference between God's promises and any we might make?

DAY 41
More to explore

KEYPOINT
Paul sets an example of thanks and prayer for others.

Today's passages are:
Table Talk: Ephesians 1v15-17
XTB: Ephesians 1v15-19

Get together some of the symbols and objects to do with the last five days and recap some of the things learnt. (E.g. best friends picture; a wrapped present; two pieces of string; treasure map; a cross; a sealed letter.)

Paul starts this next part of Ephesians, "For this reason ...". He is saying that because of all the things we've learnt over the last five days, he does something... **Read Ephesians 1v15-17** (Check out Day 38 for what 'revelation' means.)

Paul gave thanks for the Christians at Ephesus. What exactly does he thank God for? (v15) (Their faith and their love.) What does he pray for them? (v17) (That the Spirit will make them wise and reveal God to them.) Why does he pray for this for them? (v17) (So they will know God better.)

The things Paul has written are true for all Christians. Think of two friends who you could thank God for because of their faith in Jesus and love for others. Think of two friends who you could pray for, so they would know God better.

Pray for your friends.

Building up
Sometimes it is hard being a Christian but **Ephesians 1v19-20** tells us how and why we can keep going. What do we have? (v19) (God's power) And what is it the same as? (v20) (It is the same power that raised Jesus from the dead.) How does that make you feel?

DAY 42
Power trip

KEYPOINT
God used His power for the benefit of everyone who believes and trusts in Jesus.

Today's passages are:
Table Talk: Ephesians 1v19-23
XTB: Ephesians 1v19-23

TABLE TALK

(*You need paper and pencil.*) Imagine you have the power to do <u>anything</u> (the same power as God) for one day. What would you do? Make a chart, headed "Power", with two columns. Title the first column, "My Power", and list the things you would do.

READ

Most of us would be quite selfish if we had God's power for a day, but God is very different. He is unselfish. He uses His power to help us.

Read Ephesians 1v19-23
(*Some hard ideas here—we'll just pick out a few key ones.*)

TALK

• How did God show His great power in Jesus? (*v20—raised Him from the dead.*)

• Who does Jesus rule over? (*v21—all powers in heaven and earth.*)

• What does Jesus rule over? (*v22—everything.*)

• Who does Jesus help? (*v22—the church, us.*)

Put these answers in your "Power" chart in the <u>second</u> column, titled, "God's Power".

DO

Praise God for the power He's given Jesus for our benefit.

PRAY

Building up
In v23, Paul says the church (Christians) is Christ's body. **Read 1 Corinthians 12v12-27**, to see how important <u>every</u> part of the body of Jesus is. That's all of us who believe and trust in Jesus!

BEFORE AND AFTER
Below is a short summary of the situation each of us is in <u>before</u> and <u>after</u> accepting what Jesus has done through His death on the cross and resurrection from the dead. The Bible makes each of these clear.

BEFORE   *We are:*
• Dead in sin – This is the situation EVERYONE is in, relating to God.

• Facing God's anger – God cannot stand sin. He gets angry because it separates people, whom He loves, from Him. He MUST punish those who won't deal with their sin and rebellion.

• Following the ways of the world – We rebel against God's instructions and standards and instead, are influenced by the standards and ways of living set by those around us.

• God's enemy – If we are not FOR God, we are AGAINST Him. There is no in-between.

• Slaves to the devil – If we are not in God's family, the devil is our master, whether we realise it or not.

• Selfish in doing what we want – We think we are rulers of our own lives, making our own decisions. But although some things may work out, many things will go wrong.

AFTER   *We are:*
• Alive in Jesus – This means we are alive spiritually and have a relationship with God, as members of His family.

• Shown God's mercy and saved by God – We will no longer have to be punished, as we deserve.

• Able to stand up for Jesus and follow His example – Realising all that God has done for us through Jesus, we live our lives to please Him.

• God's children – This is the promise that we have from God. It is not a 'maybe', but a 'definitely'.

• Free in Jesus to love and serve – Instead of being slaves and tied up, we are free to do all the things God wants us to, especially to love and serve other people.

DAY 43
Before...

KEYPOINT
Paul reminds the Ephesians what they were like before they followed Jesus.

Today's passages are:
Table Talk: Ephesians 2v1-3
XTB: Ephesians 2v1-3

DO

Dress up as *scruffy* as you can. Put on clothes that don't match and even mess up your hair (if you've got some!). How would you feel going to meet the Queen like this? Would they let you in?

READ

Today's passage is a bit like you dressing scruffy for the Queen—but it's to do with your life stopping you being God's friend.
Read Ephesians 2v1-3

TALK

What were the Ephesians like because of their sins? (v1) (*Dead*) They weren't physically dead, but it means they were separated from God and the eternal life He gives. Whose ways did they follow? (v2) (*The world's and the devil's.*)

THINK

What kind of things do we do which are not God's ways? These things make us God's enemies. What will we face? (v3) (*God's anger/wrath.*)

But remember that Jesus came to save us from God's anger at sin. More about that tomorrow.

PRAY

Ask God to help you to live His way and say sorry for the things which you know you have done wrong.

Building up
Think of some things which you could do to show people that you follow God's way and not the world's. Make sure that you do some of these over the next few days.

DAY 44
Amazing grace

KEYPOINT
God's love has saved us even though we don't deserve it.

Today's passages are:
Table Talk: Ephesians 2v4-6
XTB: Ephesians 2v4-10

TABLE TALK

Dress as *smart* as you can—we will say why later. *Look back to Day 38 and Notes to Parents to check out the explanation for* **Grace** *and* **Mercy**.

READ

Remember how we left the Ephesians yesterday... dead in their sins, following the devil's and the world's ways, and being separated from God. Today we see how things can change.
Read Ephesians 2v4-6

TALK

What does Paul say we are? (v5) (*Alive in Christ.*) That sounds much better than being dead in our sins! What three things have made this possible? (v4-5) (*God's love, mercy and grace.*) Where does God raise us to? (v6) (*Sits us with Jesus.*)

THINK

Today, wearing our smartest clothes, gives us a picture of what God does for us. God loves us so much that He makes us clean from all the wrong things in us and makes us a new person. The picture of us sitting with Jesus in heaven means we will go to heaven and live with Him forever.

PRAY

It's God who deserves the praise! If you are a Christian, thank Him for saving you.

Building up
Read Ephesians 2v8-10 What do the verses say being saved is? (v8) (*God's gift*) So, what can't we do? (v9) (*boast*)

Verse 10 says we are created like Jesus to do good things. Think of some of the things you could do for others and plan to do them.

DAY 45 Wallbreaker, peacemaker

Today's passages are:
Table Talk: Ephesians 2v14-16
XTB: Ephesians 2v14-18

TABLE TALK

Get two chairs and a blanket and make a barrier between you. Crouch down and without speaking try to communicate through the barrier.

READ

This passage is talking about a <u>barrier</u> between Jews and Gentiles (everyone who isn't a Jew). It wasn't like a physical wall. It was a barrier caused by the hate they had for each other.
Read Ephesians 2v14-16

TALK

Who brought peace between Jews and Gentiles? (v14) (*Jesus*) What has happened to the barrier? (v14) (*Destroyed.*) How has Jesus brought peace? (v16) (*By dying on the cross.*) What was His purpose? (v15) (*To bring them together as a new people and to bring them peace with God.*)

DO

Pull the blanket down and lay a picture of the cross (or your Bible) over the blanket to show what Jesus has done.

PRAY

Thank God for breaking all barriers down through Jesus and bringing peace. Ask Him to help you keep peace with others.

Building up
Read Ephesians 2v17-18. It says Jesus preached peace to the Jews (those near) and the Gentiles (those far away). What has this given us? (v18) (*Access to God. We have this especially through prayer.*) What could you pray to God about?

DAY 46 You belong

Today's passages are:
Table Talk: Ephesians 2v19-22
XTB: Ephesians 2v19-22

TABLE TALK

Talk about being on holiday in another country. What is it like? What are the good things and the bad things?

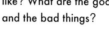

READ

Being in another country is strange and can be difficult to cope with. Paul says the Ephesians <u>were</u> like foreigners in another country. But now, because of all that Jesus has done, the Ephesians are no longer foreigners, but members of God's family.
Read Ephesians 2v19-22

TALK

Because of Jesus, those who believe in Him belong in God's family, rather than being strangers or foreigners. How does Paul describe them? (v21) (*A building becoming a temple.*) Paul says we are like a building where the Holy Spirit lives. (v22).

DO

(*Optional*) Draw a church building using big bricks. Now draw a different face on each brick. Across the bottom write out verse 22.

If we are being built together, how should we treat each other? What can you do to help others in God's family?

PRAY

Thank God that Jesus makes us part of God's new people. Ask him to help you to treat others in his family with kindness.

Building up
Read **Ephesians 2v20** again. What is the foundation built of? (*Built on apostles and prophets teaching with Jesus as the cornerstone.*) Remember you are like a brick in God's building, the church. If Jesus is the cornerstone—the most important part of God's people—we won't fall apart.

DAY 47
Grace at work

KEYPOINT
Paul shares God's mystery (secret plan), because the Holy Spirit has revealed it to him.

Today's passages are:
Table Talk: Ephesians 3v4-6
XTB: Ephesians 3v1-7

TABLE TALK

Have you ever managed to work out a mystery, a secret plan or a problem? Talk about what it was and how you felt when you had solved it.

READ

Paul has been teaching some 'big' ideas in Ephesians, and here is another one. **Read Ephesians 3v4–6** to find out more.

TALK

Who is the mystery about? (v4) (*Jesus*) Who has made it known to Paul? (v5) (*The Holy Spirit.*) What is the mystery? (*Fill in these four missing words below: Jesus, Jews, Gentiles, God's.*)

> G_____ can be part of
>
> G_____ people as well as J_____
>
> because J_____ died.

Paul says this is the <u>Gospel</u> of God's <u>grace</u>. (*Look up Day 38 Notes for Parents for the meaning of both those words.*)

THINK

If Paul says Gentiles <u>and</u> Jews can be part of God's people, then who can be in God's family today? (*Anyone can be.*) How should this affect your attitude to everyone around you?

PRAY

Grace is God's HUGE kindness to people who don't deserve it. People like you and me! Thank God for His grace.

Building up
God accepts everyone, but <u>we</u> don't always do the same! **Read Luke 10v27–37** about the Good Samaritan and answer the question in v29 for yourself.

DAY 48
Part of a plan

KEYPOINT
God's people, the church, now make known the wisdom of God.

Today's passages are:
Table Talk: Ephesians 3v8-10
XTB: Ephesians 3v8-13

TABLE TALK

Get a newspaper or magazine and look at the pictures of different people. Decide who God would want in His family, (the church), and who He wouldn't. Say why you made each decision.

READ

God makes all sorts of different people His friends through Jesus. People who wouldn't normally be friends with each other. **Read Ephesians 3v8-10** to see why.

TALK

Paul is writing about his special privilege of telling people about Jesus. Who did he tell the good news about Jesus to? (v8) (*Gentiles/non-Jews.*) Who did he tell about God's mystery/secret plan? (v9) (*Everyone.*) *Check back to yesterday to see what this mystery was.*

God uses His people, the church, to show how wise He is and to show that His plan is happening. Who else is this wisdom being shown to? (v10) (*To teach unseen angelic rulers of God's great plan.*)

THINK

Paul wouldn't let anything stop him from telling anyone and everyone about Jesus. He didn't choose who to tell. Do you? Follow Paul's example.

PRAY

Ask God to help you to tell others about Him even when it is hard and they don't look like they will listen.

Building up
Read Ephesians 3v12. What have we got through Jesus living in us and because of our faith in Him? (*Boldness to go into God's presence.*) How do we do this? (*Through prayer.*) Talk to God about everything—because He wants us to.

DAY 49
Get praying

Today's passages are:
Table Talk: Ephesians 3v14-19
XTB: Ephesians 3v14-19

TABLE TALK

Before beginning today, spend a few minutes doing some fitness training. Start with running on the spot, followed by some press-ups and some sit-ups. Well done!

READ

We often spend time building our muscles up and getting <u>physically</u> fit, but the last two weeks have been about getting <u>spiritually</u> fit.
Read Ephesians 3v14-19

TALK

What a great passage and summary, full of God's love! Paul prays that God will strengthen them, by Jesus living in their hearts. What does Paul pray for in v18? (*They would understand Jesus' love.*)

How does Paul explain the hugeness of Jesus' love in v18-19? (*It is wide and long, high and deep, and bigger than we could ever understand.*) **WOW!**

THINK

Paul was praying for the Ephesian Church, but what should <u>we</u> do as a result of this passage? (*Pray for everyone in our church in the same way as Paul.*)

PRAY

Ask God to make you so full of Jesus' love that the things you do & say make others want to know more about Him.

Building up
Think about building up your Christian life all the time. What must you keep doing? (*Read your Bible, pray and meet with other Christians.*) Tell a friend about what you have been learning.

DAY 50
A glorious ending

Today's passages are:
Table Talk: Ephesians 3v20-21
XTB: Ephesians 3v20-21

TABLE TALK

Think about some of the things you are really good at. Mime them to each other and see if you can guess what they are.

READ

When we can do things, especially difficult things, sometimes we can be praised by others. They say, we should 'enjoy the glory'. As we finish the first half of Ephesians, **read chapter 3v20-21** and see who gets the praise and the glory.

TALK

What does Paul believe God can do? (v20-21) (*Anything, everything and more.*) How long should we bring glory and praise to God? (v21) (*Forever and ever.*)

DO

Make a card to God, saying thank you for some of the things you have learnt from Ephesians chapters 1-3.

PRAY

Read Ephesians 3v20-21 again, as a prayer.

Building up
Read **Ephesians 3v20** again. What does it say God is able to do in us? (*Immeasurably MORE than all we ask or imagine!*) Spend a few minutes thinking and imagining what God could do in you, so that others would praise God.

DAYS 51-65
Notes for Parents

THE BOOK OF NUMBERS

(*You will need three pieces of paper and a pencil.*) Write **Past**, **Present** and **Future** on the paper as shown:

Past	Present	Future

<u>Note:</u> *Past* means before the time of Numbers, *Present* is during Numbers, and *Future* looks forward to what will happen after Numbers.

INTRODUCTION

God had made three amazing promises to the Israelites. As we return to the book of **Numbers**, we're going to see how God is keeping those promises.
Read about them below:

1 LAND → God promised to give the Israelites the land of Canaan to live in.

2 CHILDREN → God said that the Israelite nation would be so HUGE that there would be too many to count!

3 BLESSING ↘ God promised that someone from the Israelite nation would be God's way of blessing the whole world.

Please return to **Table Talk** to see how God keeps those promises.

Building up

In the book of Numbers, the Israelites are on their way to the promised land of Canaan. Jump back to **Exodus 3v7-8** to see what God told Moses it would be like. (God was speaking to Moses from a burning bush.)

DAY 51
Past, present, future

KEYPOINT
God kept all of His amazing promises to the Israelites—land, children and blessing.

Today's passages are:
Table Talk: Numbers 1v46
XTB: Numbers 1v46 & Exodus 3v7-8

TABLE TALK
Please start today's Table Talk with **Notes for Parents** opposite.

ONE

<u>PAST</u> At the beginning of Numbers, God told Moses to count the Israelites. Moses counted all the men who were old enough to fight in the army. There were a lot of them! **Read Numbers 1v46**

How many men were there? (603,550) If you add the women and children, there were probably over **Two Million Israelites!!** <u>Draw</u> lots of stick men under **Past** to show that God had kept His promise to make them a huge nation.

TWO

<u>PRESENT</u> In Numbers the Israelites are travelling to the promised land of Canaan. God gave them something to follow, so that they would know where and when to travel. What was it? (A cloud—Numbers 10v11-13.) On the **Present** sheet, <u>draw</u> some stick men (walking) following a cloud, to show that God was keeping His promise to lead them to Canaan.

THREE

<u>FUTURE</u> The third promise (Blessing) hadn't happened yet. It was still well over 1000 years in the future! They would have to <u>trust</u> God to keep that promise too. But *we* know that God <u>did</u> keep that third promise. Who did God send as His way of blessing the whole world? (*Jesus*) <u>Draw</u> a cross under Future, to show how God kept His third promise.

PRAY
Thank God for sending Jesus as His way of blessing the whole world.

Building up
See **Notes for Parents** opposite.

DAY 52
I spy...

Today's passages are:
Table Talk: Numbers 13v17-20 & 23
XTB: Numbers 13v1-25

TABLE TALK

Collect any fruit you have. Which is heaviest? (*You can use scales, or just feel the weight in your hands.*)

READ

The Israelites are now <u>very close</u> to Canaan. So God tells Moses to send twelve men to check out the land. Listen to see what these *twelve spies* had to find out about.
Read Numbers 13v17-20

TALK

What were they to find out about the people? (v18) (*Weak or strong, few or many.*) About the towns? (v19) (*Fortified or not.*) About the land? (v20) (*Fertile soil, with trees?*)

Moses also told them to bring back some <u>fruit</u>. **Read Numbers 13v23**

What fruit did they bring back? (*Grapes, pomegranates, figs.*) The bunch of grapes was enormously heavy. How did they carry it? (*On a pole.*)

PRAY

God had promised them a **good** land, full of fab food—and it was! Thank God that He <u>always</u> keeps His promises.

Building up
The twelve spies were leaders from the twelve tribes of Israel. One of them was going to be the next leader of the Israelites. Do you know which one? (*See v8 & v16.*) We'll find out more about him on Day 62.

DAY 53
We can do it!

Today's passages are:
Table Talk: Numbers 13v30-33
XTB: Numbers 13v25-33

TABLE TALK

Moses has sent **twelve spies** to check out the land of Canaan. Read the cartoon story in **Notes for Parents** (on the next page) to see what kind of news they brought back. (*With older children, also read the report in Numbers 13v26-29.*)

What was the **good** news? (*The land was <u>fabulous</u>, as God had promised.*) But what was the **bad** news? (*The cities were <u>strong</u> and the people were <u>tall</u>.*)

READ

Now that the spies have given their report, the rest of the Israelites have to decide who to trust.
Read Numbers 13v30-33

TALK

<u>Caleb</u> trusted God. What did he say they should do? (*See v30.*) We know from later on (e.g. 14v6) that <u>Joshua</u> believed this too. But the other ten spies didn't! What did they do? (v32) (*Spread a bad report.*)

THINK

Now the Israelites had to decide who to trust. Would they trust **God** (who had promised to give them this land)? Or would they believe the **ten spies** (who said they couldn't fight the people)? Who do you <u>think</u> they will trust? Why? (*More tomorrow.*)

Imagine that you were there. Who do you think <u>you</u> would have trusted? Why?

PRAY

Deuteronomy 31v6 says, "The LORD will not fail you or abandon you." Thank God that He is like this.

Building up
Think of at least three reasons why you can trust God.

Notes for Parents

THE TWELVE SPIES
The Israelites had nearly reached Canaan. So Moses sent twelve spies to check out the land...

Based on Numbers 13v17-33

True or false?

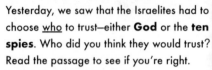

KEYPOINT
The Israelites didn't trust God to bring them safely into Canaan. They rebelled against Him.

Today's passages are:
Table Talk: Numbers 14v1-4
XTB: Numbers 14v1-10

TABLE TALK
Read the cartoon story again to remind yourselves about what's happened so far.

READ
Yesterday, we saw that the Israelites had to choose <u>who</u> to trust—either **God** or the **ten spies**. Who did you think they would trust? Read the passage to see if you're right.
Read Numbers 14v1-4

TALK
The Israelites <u>didn't</u> trust God! What did they think would happen if they went into Canaan? (v3) (*The men would be killed, the women and children captured.*) What did they want to do instead? (v4) (*Choose a new leader and go back to Egypt.*)

THINK
What a <u>terrible</u> thing to say! It showed they were turning their backs on God and on all that He had done for them. Why? (**God** was their King. **God** had chosen their leader, Moses. **God** had rescued them from Egypt. **God** had promised to give them a new land.) The Israelites were <u>rebelling</u> against all that God had done.

Joshua and Caleb were horrified! They begged the Israelites not to turn away from God. But they wouldn't listen! Instead, they talked about <u>killing</u> Joshua and Caleb. (*We'll find out what happened tomorrow.*)

PRAY
The Bible tells us that we can <u>always</u> trust God. Ask Him to help you to do that.

Building up
Read what Joshua and Caleb said in **Numbers 14v5-10**. Find <u>three</u> things they believed that God would do. (See v8-9) The people in Canaan really were tall and strong, so why were Joshua and Caleb so confident? (v9) (*They knew that **God** was with them.*)

Two-headed coin

> **KEYPOINT**
> God is both **just** and **merciful**.

Today's passages are:
Table Talk: Numbers 14v20
XTB: Numbers 14v10-20

 DO

Make a large coin out of a circle of paper or card. Fill in the two sides of the coin as shown in **Notes for Parents**.

Today we see two sides of God's character. They seem quite different, but both have to be there—like the two sides of the same coin...

 MERCY

God is Merciful (*Show the mercy side of the coin.*) Think of some ways that God has shown *mercy* to the Israelites. (*E.g. Rescued them from Egypt, brought them safely across the desert to the edge of Canaan—even though they moaned so much!*)

 JUSTICE

God is Just (*Show the justice side of the coin.*) The Israelites have just done something very wrong. What was it? (*Turned their backs on God and all He'd done for them.*) God was <u>angry</u> with them. He said He would punish their sin by destroying them all, as they deserved. (Numbers 14v11-12)

 MERCY

God is Merciful (*Show the mercy side.*) Moses begged God not to destroy the Israelites. **Read Numbers 14v20** What did God do? (*Forgave them.*)

 JUSTICE

God is Just (*Show the justice side.*) Because God is <u>just</u>, He had to punish their sin. So He told them they would not go into Canaan. Instead they would spend another <u>40 years</u> in the desert!

Prayer ideas in **Notes for Parents**.

Building up
Read Moses' prayer in **Numbers 14v13-20**. Verse 18 echoes God's own words to Moses in **Exodus 34v5-8**. Thank God that He is like this.

Notes for Parents

GOD'S CHARACTER

God is both merciful and just. He is both at the same time—like the two sides of one coin...

Make your own coin, as shown:

GOD IS MERCIFUL

Mercy means to show someone kindness that they don't deserve.

GOD IS JUST

Justice means making sure that sin is punished and good is rewarded.

PRAY

THINK AND PRAY

God is Just
<u>Everyone</u> sins. Because God is just, He must punish that sin.

God is Merciful
God sent Jesus to take the punishment <u>we</u> deserve, so that we can be forgiven.

**God is both just and merciful.
Thank Him!**

DAY 56
Too late to turn back

TABLE TALK

Use yesterday's coin to recap the story so far:
Mercy—God brought the Israelites to Canaan; **Justice**—When the Israelites turned away from God, He said He would destroy them; **Mercy**—when Moses begged God to forgive the Israelites, He did; **Justice**—God said they would spend the next 40 years in the desert.

During those 40 years, everyone who hadn't trusted God would die. Only the few who trusted Him—like Joshua and Caleb—would live to go to Canaan.

READ

The Israelites didn't like the sound of that! So they changed their minds about going into the promised land.
Read Numbers 14v39-45

TALK

What did Moses tell the people? (v42) (*"Don't go, God isn't with you."*) But they went anyway! What happened? (v45) (*Their enemies beat them.*)

THINK

The people were finally obeying God's original command. But only because they didn't like His new instructions! They were still doing what **they** thought was best instead of obeying **God**.

PRAY

Do you ever do what you think is best instead of obeying God? Say sorry, and ask Him to help you to trust Him more.

Building up
Read v44 again. What didn't go with them? (*The ark and Moses.*) The ark reminded the Israelites that they were God's people, and that He was with them. But this time the ark wasn't with them. What should they have realised? (*That God wasn't with them—see v42.*)

DAY 57
Soggy saga

TABLE TALK

Pour a glass of water, and put it where you can all see it. How long did it take to get it? (*Probably less than a minute.*) Now imagine that you're walking through the **desert**, like the Israelites. Where would you get water from? (*Carry it from your last water source e.g. an oasis.*)

READ

We're jumping forward to chapter 20 of Numbers, where the Israelites are grumbling again. They have run out of water, and they're blaming Moses and Aaron. **Read Numbers 20v7-11**

TALK

What did God tell Moses to do? (v8) (*Speak to the rock.*) Moses spoke to the people, then hit the rock twice with his staff.

Draw what happened. (v11)

THINK

The Israelites were a terrible lot of moanalots! Did they deserve God's kindness? (*No!*) But yet again, God was **merciful** to them.

PRAY

God was kind to the Israelites even though they didn't deserve it. We don't deserve His kindness either. So spend some time thanking Him for it!

Building up
Read about the Israelites' moans in **Numbers 20v1-5**. Who are they blaming? (v2-3) But whose fault is it really that they are in the desert? (Numbers 14v34-35) Notice that the fruit they are longing for in 20v5, is the same fruit the spies found in Canaan! (13v23)

DAY 58
Sad saga

TABLE TALK

Ask your child to tell you yesterday's story. (The Israelites grumbled about having no water, God told Moses to speak to the rock, Moses hit the rock twice with his staff, water gushed out.)

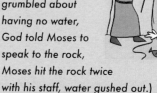

READ

What had God told Moses to do? (*Speak to the rock—v8*) But Moses <u>didn't</u> do what God had said...
Read Numbers 20v9-12

TALK

God told Moses to <u>speak</u> to the rock, but what did Moses actually do? (v11) (*Hit the rock twice.*) Moses was a good leader, who trusted God. But he wasn't **perfect**! This time, Moses <u>didn't</u> obey God's command.

THINK

By the way—only <u>one</u> man has ever lived a perfect life. Who? (*Jesus*)

Yesterday we saw that God was **merciful** to the Israelites. But what's the other side of the coin? (*God is just.*) Because God is **just**, He punished Moses for his sin. How? (v12) (*Moses would not go with the Israelites into the promised land.*)

PRAY

Say sorry to God for times when <u>you</u> have disobeyed Him. Ask Him to help you always to trust Him and obey Him.

Building up
Does this story remind you of another one? Something very similar happened in Exodus. **Read Exodus 17v1-7**. That time, God <u>did</u> tell Moses to strike the rock—and Moses obeyed Him completely.

DAY 59
Saved by a snake?

DO

If you can, **make a model** of a snake on a pole. (E.g. a pipe cleaner wrapped round a stick or straw.) Otherwise, **draw a picture** of it, as shown.

READ

The Israelites were moaning again. They complained about the food God gave them, and grumbled at God.
Read Numbers 21v6-9

TALK

How did God punish the Israelites? (v6) (*With poisonous snakes.*) The Israelites knew they had <u>sinned</u>, so they asked Moses to pray for them. What did God tell Moses to do? (v8) (*Make a snake on a pole.*) If anyone was bitten, what did they have to do? (v8) (*Look at the bronze snake on the pole.*) Did this save them? (v9) (*Yes*)

THINK

Because God is **just**, He sent the snakes to <u>punish</u> the Israelites.
Because God is **merciful**, He gave them a way to be <u>saved</u>.

PRAY

Thank God that He is always both just and merciful.

Building up
Why were the Israelites saved when they looked at the bronze snake—was it because the snake had special powers? (*No!*) Read God's words in **verse 8** again. Why were the people saved? (*Because they <u>trusted</u> what God said, and turned to the rescue He provided.*)

DAY 60
Saved by Jesus

KEYPOINT
We deserve to be punished for our sin. God provided a way to be rescued—through Jesus.

Today's passages are:
Table Talk: John 3v14-16
XTB: John 3v14-16

TABLE TALK

Use yesterday's model or picture to recap the story of the snake on a pole.

Jesus used this story to teach us about Himself. **Read John 3v14-16**

TALK

What was lifted up in the desert? (*The snake on a pole.*) In John 3, Jesus says that someone else will be lifted up. Who? (v14) (*Jesus—"Son of Man" is a title Jesus often used for Himself. He was "lifted up" on the cross.*) What did Jesus say would be given to everyone who believes in Him? (v15) (*Eternal life.*)

DO

Write out two lists as shown. Talk through each part with your child as you write it.

The Israelites	Us
• They sinned.	• We <u>all</u> sin.
• They were punished.	• We deserve to be punished.
• God provided a way to be rescued.	• God provided a way to be rescued.

THINK

<u>The Israelites</u> had to turn to the snake to be saved. <u>We</u> must turn to Jesus, and put our trust in Him as our Rescuer.

Read John 3v16 aloud.

PRAY
Thank God for sending Jesus to die in your place so that you can be forgiven.

Building up
It wasn't the bronze snake that saved the Israelites, it was <u>God</u>. But later they seem to have forgotten this, and started to worship the snake! **Read 2 Kings 18v1-4** Ask God to help not to make the same mistake. Your thanks and praise belong to **Him**—not anything else!

DAY 61
Journey's end

KEYPOINT
After 40 years in the desert, everyone who <u>hadn't</u> trusted God had died, just as He said.

Today's passages are:
Table Talk: Numbers 26v51
XTB: Numbers 26v51 & 62-65

READ

At the beginning of Numbers, Moses took a census, and counted all the men. There were 603,500 of them. (Numbers 1v46) At the end of Numbers, Moses took another census. **Read Numbers 26v51**

TALK

How many men were there this time? (601,730)

There's a gap of **40 years** between the first and second census. During that time the Israelites wandered around the desert. Do you remember why? (*They hadn't trusted God to bring them safely to Canaan, so He punished them.*) During those years, everyone who <u>hadn't</u> trusted God died—just as He said they would.

DO

At the end of the 40 years, the Israelites reached **Moab**. *Draw their winding path through the desert, starting at **Mount Sinai**, and ending in **Moab**.*

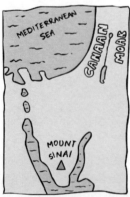

PRAY
Everything happened just as God had said it would. Thank God that His words <u>always</u> come true.

Building up
God took special care of the Israelites in those 40 years. **See Deuteronomy 8v4!**

DAY 62 New leader, same God

Today's passages are:
Table Talk: Deuteronomy 31v1-8
XTB: Deuteronomy 31v1-8

TABLE TALK

Mental maths: See if your child can do these sums in their head. 90 + 30; 40 X 3; 200 - 80; 240 − 2. (*The answer should always be 120.*)

READ

Guess how old Moses is now! (*120!*) He knows that he won't lead the Israelites into the promised land of Canaan. Instead, they will have a **new** leader. **Read Deuteronomy 31v1-8**.

TALK

Who would be the new leader? (*Joshua*) What do you know about Joshua? (*He was one of the two spies who did trust God—Num 14v6-8.*)
Verse 3 says that Joshua will take the Israelites into Canaan. Who else will go with them? (v3) (*God*)

THINK

The Israelites will have a **new leader**. But it will be the **same God** who goes with them! So they have no need to be afraid. God will never let them down!

DO

Copy verse 6 onto some paper. Put it where you will all see it each day.

PRAY

If you are a Christian, then this promise is for you too. How does that make you feel? Talk to God about it.

Building up
You can divide Moses' life into three chunks of 40 years each. Check out parts of Stephen's speech in Acts 7 to see what happened in each chunk. **Read Acts 7v23, v30 & v36**. (*Or the whole story in Acts 7v20-38.*)

DAY 63 A people saved by God

Today's passages are:
Table Talk: Deuteronomy 33v29
XTB: Deuteronomy 33v29

TABLE TALK

Write the names of the first five books of the Bible on five strips of paper. Ask your child to try to put them in the correct order. Get them to check their answer in the contents page of their Bible.

READ

The last of these five books is called **Deuteronomy**, which means "second law". In this book, Moses tells the Israelites God's law for the second time. Read the very last of his words:
Read Deuteronomy 33v29

TALK

What does Moses say the Israelites are? (*A people saved by God.*) They weren't like anyone else. They were **unique**! Not because they were especially good (we know they weren't!), but because they'd been **chosen** and **saved** by God.

THINK

Read the above paragraph again, and see if this sounds like any other people you can think of.

PRAY

Who else can be called a people chosen and saved by God? (*Christians*) If you are a Christian, then you have been chosen and saved by God too. **Not** because you've been especially good! But because Jesus died for you as your Rescuer. Thank God for this!

Building up
Read what Peter wrote about this in **1 Peter 2v9-10**. Thank God for His great mercy (v10). Ask Him to help you to tell others about Him (v9).

DAY 64
Looking on

> **KEYPOINT**
> God showed Moses the promised land of Canaan, before Moses died.

Today's passages are:
Table Talk : Deuteronomy 34v1-9
XTB : Deuteronomy 34v1-9

TABLE TALK

What's the highest place you've stood? (*The top of a tower, or bridge, or hill?*) What could you see from the top?

READ

When Moses had finished teaching the Israelites, he climbed to the top of a nearby mountain. From there, God showed him the whole of the promised land.
Read Deuteronomy 34v4-9

TALK

Moses died on the mountain, having seen the promised land of Canaan. Who buried Moses? (v6) (*God did.*) Who became the new leader of the Israelites? (v9) (*Joshua*)

THINK

The books of Numbers and Deuteronomy teach us about God's character. Think of some words to describe Him, and try to link each one with an event from the life of Moses. (*E.g. God is <u>powerful</u>—He provided manna for the Israelites for 40 years; God is <u>faithful</u>—He kept His promise to bring them to Canaan; God is <u>merciful</u>—He...*)

PRAY

Thank God for the things you've learnt about Him. Ask Him to help you to get to know Him even better as you continue to read the Bible together.

Building up
Think back over the life of Moses. Do you want to be like him? In what ways?

DAY 65
The promise-keeper

> **KEYPOINT**
> All of God's promises came true when God sent **Jesus**.

Today's passages are:
Table Talk : Deuteronomy 34v10-12
XTB : Deuteronomy 34v10-12

TABLE TALK

What's the title of this book? (*The Promise Keeper.*) Why do you think I've chosen this title? (*The picture on the front cover gives a clue.*)

READ

Read Deuteronomy 34v10-12

How many other people were there like Moses? (*None!*) What was unique about him? (*v10—God spoke with him face to face, v11-12—he performed miracles.*)

TALK

Moses was a **prophet** (God's messenger) and a great leader. But earlier in Deuteronomy God had promised to send <u>another</u> prophet. (Deut 18v15+18) This prophet would be far greater than Moses. Who do you think he was? (*Jesus*)

THINK

Look how God kept His promises:
* God promised to send a new **King**. —Who did He send? (*Jesus*)

* God promised to send a **Rescuer**. —Who did He send? (*Jesus*)

* God promised to send someone to be His way of **blessing** the whole world. —Who did He send? (*Jesus*)

* And God promised to send a **prophet** like Moses. Who did He send? (*Jesus!*)

PRAY

God promised that Jesus would come—and He did! He came as **Prophet**, **King**, **Rescuer**, to **bless** the whole world—just as God had said. Thank God, the Promise-Keeper, for sending Jesus.

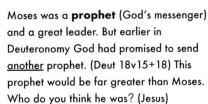

Building up
Read **Psalm 103**. (*All of it if you have time, otherwise v6-14.*) This great poem shows us wh[at] God is like. Which of these characteristics have you seen while reading Numbers and Deuteronomy?

Extra Readings

WHY ARE THERE EXTRA READINGS?

Table Talk and XTB both come out every three months. The main Bible reading pages contain material for 65 days. That's enough to use them Monday to Friday for three months.

Many families find that their routine is different at weekends from during the week. Some find that regular Bible reading fits in well on school days, but not at weekends. Others encourage their children to read the Bible for themselves during the week, then explore the Bible together as a family at weekends, when there's more time to do the activities together.

The important thing is to help your children get into the habit of reading the Bible for themselves—and that they see that regular

Bible reading is important for **you** as well.

If you **are** able to read the Bible with your children every day, that's great! The extra readings on the next page will augment the main Table Talk pages so that you have enough material to cover the full three months.

You could:

- Read Table Talk every day for 65 days, then use the extra readings for the rest of the third month.

- Read Table Talk on weekdays. Use the extra readings at weekends.

- Use any other combination that works for your family.

TIME TO PRAY...

Do you find praying difficult? Do you wonder what to say? Or what to pray about? In these extra readings we're going to see what the Bible says about prayer.

There are 26 Bible readings on the next three pages. Part of each verse has been printed for you—but with a word missing. Fill in the missing words as you read the verses. Then see if you can find them all in the wordsearch.

Note: Some are written backwards—or diagonally!!

E	B	F	S	H	E	P	H	E	R	D	T	E	T	F
A	A	O	K	W	O	R	R	Y	B	E	H	V	R	A
R	G	R	E	A	T	A	O	T	A	E	A	O	O	I
N	O	G	L	O	R	Y	X	C	K	D	N	L	U	T
E	O	I	B	Y	E	E	H	A	N	S	K	M	B	H
S	D	V	N	I	A	R	A	T	O	S	F	A	L	F
T	K	E	X	T	B	G	O	D	W	I	U	R	E	U
L	N	D	A	Y	S	G	N	I	K	N	L	Y	Y	L
Y	O	U	R	P	E	O	P	L	E	G	R	G	P	N
T	W	O	C	C	A	S	I	O	N	I	A	N	P	E
A	L	T	R	U	M	P	E	T	S	N	I	I	A	S
G	E	T	H	S	E	M	A	N	E	G	N	K	H	S

Extra Readings

1 ☐ Read Mark 1v35

If you have a busy day—how about getting up early to pray? Jesus did!

"Very e _ _ _ _
in the morning, long before daylight,
Jesus got up and left the house.
He went out to a lonely place,
where He prayed." (v35)

2 ☐ Read Philippians 4v6-7

We can pray about everything. We don't need to worry.

"Don't W _ _ _ _ about anything, but in all your prayers ask God for what you need, always asking Him with a thankful heart."(v6)

3 ☐ Read Ephesians 6v18

We can pray at all times, wherever we are or whatever we are doing.

"Pray on every O _ _ _ _ _ _ _ _
as the Spirit leads." (v18)

4 ☐ Read Colossians 4v2

Keep on praying. Don't give up!

"Be persistent in p _ _ _ _ _
and keep alert as you pray, giving thanks to God."(v2)

5 ☐ Read 1 Thessalonians 5v16-18

We can pray to God anywhere, any time. There's loads to thank Him for, even when things seem hard.

"Be joyful always, pray at all times,
be t _ _ _ _ _ _ _ _ in all circumstances."
(v16-18)

6 ☐ Read Psalm 139v1-6

God knows all about us before we pray, and He knows what we'll say.

"LORD, you have examined me and you
K _ _ _ me." (v1)

7 ☐ Read James 5v13

If you're in trouble, pray about it. If you're happy, also pray about it!—thanking and praising God.

"Is anyone among you in
t _ _ _ _ _ _ ? He should pray.
Is anyone h _ _ _ _ ?
He should sing
praises." (v13)

8 ☐ Read Colossians 4v2-4

Pray for people who tell others about Jesus. Ask God to give them opportunities to speak for Him.

"Pray also for us, that G _ _ may open a door for our message." (v3)

9 ☐ Read 1 Timothy 2v1-2

We should pray for those who lead our country.

"I urge that petitions, prayers, requests and thanksgivings be offered to God for all people; for k _ _ _ _ and all others who are in authority." (v1-2))

10 ☐ Read John 15v12

Don't worry when you don't know how or what to pray. God's Holy Spirit will help you.

"We do not k _ _ _ what we ought to pray for, but the Spirit Himself pleads with
God " (v12)

Extra Readings

11 ☐ **Read Luke 11v1-4**

Jesus taught His followers how to pray. (Often called The Lord's Prayer.)

"Lord, **t** _ _ _ _ us to pray, just as John taught his disciples." (v1)

12 ☐ **Read Psalm 117v1-2**

Sometimes prayers are very short. Read the whole of Psalm 117 (the <u>shortest</u> psalm) aloud.

"His love for us is strong and His **f** _ _ _ _ _ _ _ _ _ _ _ is eternal." (v34)

Verses giving examples of prayer

13 ☐ **Read Mark 14v32-36**

Just before He was arrested, Jesus took time to pray.

"They came to a place called **G** _ _ _ _ _ _ _ _ _ and Jesus said to His disciples, "Sit here while I pray."" (v32)

14 ☐ **Read Luke 23v33-34**

While Jesus was being crucified, He prayed for the people who did it.

"Jesus said, '**F** _ _ _ _ _ _ them, Father. They don't know what they are doing.'" (v34)

15 ☐ **Read Acts 1v14**

After the resurrection, when Jesus went up to heaven, His followers met frequently to pray together.

"They all joined together constantly in prayer, along with the women and **M** _ _ _ the mother of Jesus and with His brothers." (v14)

16 ☐ **Read Acts 12v5**

When Peter was arrested by Herod, the other Christians prayed for him. You can read about the answer to their prayers in Acts 12v6-19.

"So Peter was kept in jail, but the people of the church were praying **e** _ _ _ _ _ _ _ _ to God for him." (v5)

17 ☐ **Read Acts 16v25**

Paul and Silas were thrown in prison for teaching about Jesus. But even so, they were praying and singing!

"About midnight Paul and Silas were praying and **s** _ _ _ _ _ _ hymns to God." (v25)

18 ☐ **Read James 5v17-18**

Elijah was just like us. But look how God answered his prayer!

"Elijah was the same kind if person as we are. He prayed earnestly that there would be no **r** _ _ _ and no **r** _ _ _ fell on the land for three and a half years." (v17)

Reading Psalms aloud as prayers

19 ☐ **Read Psalm 23v1-6**

You may know a tune for this psalm. If so sing it, if not read it aloud.

"The LORD is my **s** _ _ _ _ _ _ _ ." (v1)

20 ☐ **Read Psalm 19v1-6**

Look at the sky—then praise God (He designed the sky!) for being so great. "How clearly the sky reveals God's **g** _ _ _ _ !" (v1)

Extra Readings

21 ☐ **Read Psalm 150v1-6**

If you can play an instrument, play a tune to praise God. Otherwise clap your hands as you read this psalm.

"Praise Him with t _ _ _ _ _ _ _ .
Praise Him with harps and lyres." (v3)

22 ☐ **Read Psalm 136v1**

Every line of this psalm ends with the same words, thanking God for His everlasting love.

"Give thanks to the LORD, for He is good;
His l _ _ _ is eternal." (v1)

23 ☐ **Read Psalm 47v1-9**

When we pray, we are talking to the King of the whole world!

"God is K _ _ _ over all the world." (v7)

24 ☐ **Read Psalm 100v1-5**

If we are Christians, then we are God's people. He looks after us like a shepherd takes care of his sheep.

"We are His p _ _ _ _ _ , we are His flock." (v3)

25 ☐ **Read Psalm 96v1-3**

If you're a Christian, ask God to help you to tell your friends about Him. This psalm says we should tell the whole world about God saving us.

"Proclaim His glory to the nations,
His mighty d _ _ _ _
to all peoples." (v3)

26 ☐ **Read Psalm 96v4-6**

We should praise and thank God because He is the Greatest!

"The Lord is g _ _ _ _ and is to be highly praised." (v4)

WHAT NEXT?

We hope that Table Talk has helped you get into a regular habit of reading the Bible with your children.

There are twelve issues of Table Talk available. Each issue contains 65 full Table Talk outlines, plus 26 days of extra readings.

Available from your local Good Book Company website:

UK: www.thegoodbook.co.uk
North America: www.thegoodbook.com
Australia: www.thegoodbook.com.au
New Zealand: www.thegoodbook.co.nz

THE NEXT ISSUE
Issue Six: Footprints

Issue Six of Table Talk explores the books of Mark, Joshua and Ephesians.

- Investigate who Jesus is and why He came in **Mark's** Gospel.
- The Israelites reach the promised land at last in **Joshua** —but battles await them!
- Read the end of Paul's prison letter to the **Ephesians**.